REALISTIC LOVE

Anger Workbook
Dr. Less Carter

The Father Book
Dr. Frank Minirth, Dr. Brian Newman, Dr. Paul Warren

Imperative People
Dr. Les Carter

The Intimacy Factor
Dr. David Stoop, Jan Stoop

Kids Who Carry Our Pain
Dr. Robert Hemfelt, Dr. Paul Warren

The Lies We Believe
Dr. Chris Thurman

Love Hunger: Recovery from Food Addiction
Dr. Frank Minirth, Dr. Paul Meier, Dr. Robert Hemfelt, Dr. Sharon Sneed

Love Hunger Action Plan
Dr. Sharon Sneed

The Love Hunger Weight-Loss Workbook
Dr. Frank Minirth, Dr. Paul Meier, Dr. Robert Hemfelt, Dr. Sharon Sneed

Love Is a Choice
Dr. Robert Hemfelt, Dr. Frank Minirth, Dr. Paul Meier

Love Is a Choice Workbook
Dr. Robert Hemfelt, Dr. Frank Minirth, Dr. Paul Meier, Dr. Brian Newman, Dr. Deborah Newman

Passages of Marriage Series
New Love
Realistic Love
Steadfast Love
Renewing Love
Transcendent Love

Dr. Frank and Mary Alice Minirth, Drs. Brian and Deborah Newman, Dr. Robert and Susan Hemfelt

Passages of Marriage Study Guide Series
New Love Study Guide
Realistic Love Study Guide
Steadfast Love Study Guide
Renewing Love Study Guide
Transcendent Love Study Guide
Dr. Frank and Mary Alice Minirth, Drs. Brian and Deborah Newman, Dr. Robert and Susan Hemfelt

The Path to Serenity
Dr. Robert Hemfelt, Dr. Frank Minirth, Dr. Richard Fowler, Dr. Paul Meier

Please Let Me Know You, God
Dr. Larry Stephens

The Quest
Kevin J. Brown, Ray Mitsch

Steps to a New Beginning
Sam Shoemaker, Dr. Frank Minirth, Dr. Richard Fowler, Dr. Brian Newman, Dave Carder

The Thin Disguise
Pam Vredevelt, Dr. Deborah Newman, Harry Beverly, Dr. Frank Minirth

Things That Go Bump in the Night
Dr. Paul Warren, Dr. Frank Minirth

The Truths We Must Believe
Dr. Chris Thurman

Together on a Tightrope
Dr. Richard Fowler
Rita Schweitz

Hope for the Perfectionist
Dr. David Stoop

For general information about other Minirth-Meier Clinic branch offices, counseling services, educational resources and hospital programs, call toll-free 1-800-545-1819. National Headquarters: (214)669-1733 (800)229-3000

REALISTIC LOVE

Dr. Frank and Mary Alice Minirth
Dr. Brian and Dr. Deborah Newman
Dr. Robert and Susan Hemfelt

THOMAS NELSON PUBLISHERS
NASHVILLE

The case examples presented in this book are fictional composites based on the authors' clinical experience with thousands of clients through the years. Any resemblance between these fictional characters and actual persons is coincidental. Two of the six authors, Mary Alice Minirth and Susan Hemfelt, are not psychotherapeutic clinicians and are not associated with the Minirth-Meier Clinic. The contributions of Mary Alice Minirth and Susan Hemfelt are derived from personal experience and their contribution makes no claim of professional expertise. Portions of this book that address clinical theory and clinical perspectives do not include contributions from Mary Alice Minirth and Susan Hemfelt.

Published in Nashville, Tennessee, by Thomas Nelson, Inc., and distributed in Canada by Lawson Falle, Ltd., Cambridge, Ontario.

Scripture quotations are from the NEW KING JAMES VERSION of the Bible. Copyright © 1979, 1980, 1982, Thomas Nelson, Inc., Publishers.

Library of Congress Cataloging-in-Publication Data

Realistic love : the second passage of marriage / Brian and Deborah Newman . . . [et al.].
   p.   cm.
"A Janet Thoma book"—P. 1.
ISBN 0-8407-4550-8
   1. Marriage—United States. 2. Communication in marriage—United States. I. Newman, Brian. II. Newman, Deborah.
HQ734.R282   1993
646.7'8—dc20   92-22986
                                              CIP

Printed in the United States of America
1   2   3   4   —   96   95   94   93

Contents

Acknowledgments

THE AUTHORS wish to thank the many people who helped make this book possible. Many thanks to Sandy Dengler and Catharine Walkinshaw whose writing talents brought the illustrations, thoughts, and notes from the authors to a consistent and readable form. We also thank Janet Thoma for the many hours she spent guiding, editing, and directing the completion of the manuscript. We recognize Laurie Clark and Susan Salmon for their editorial assistance and attention to the details that helped make the book complete. Last, we acknowledge our children: Rachel, Renee, Carrie, and Alicia Minirth; Rachel and Benjamin Newman; Katy, Kristin, and Robert Gray Hemfelt, for the special part they add to our passages through marriage.

Chapter 1

The Passages:
Growth Stages
of a Living Marriage

G race Katherine Chevington had seen it all. As a teen
she served in the remote pueblos of Mexico with a church
youth group, building adobe and cinderblock schoolhouses.
There she came face to face with rattlesnakes the size of a
clothes dryer vent hose. No creature is uglier than a rattlesnake.

In Irian Java she watched a shaman in red and white paint try
to kill an enemy with magic. The enemy hopped in his little
outboard motorboat and fled his island home to escape death.
As an adult, a news service correspondent, she covered wars,
earthquakes, mass murders, mall openings, state fairs, the cre-
ation of a national committee to study fungus, and a few really
juicy political campaigns. She knew firsthand the good, the bad,
the ugly, and the stupid.

And then she got married.

Grace Chevington's blue eyes and dark-haired beauty were
often compared favorably with Maria Shriver's. But the man
Grace married, Ron Reynolds, was no Arnold Schwarzenegger.
Ron, the news anchor for a small independent television fran-
chise, was certainly good-looking. His voice rumbled in a
soothing, trained baritone. He kept his beautiful hands mani-
cured to perfection, but he never did any work with them. He
was barely strong enough to put the cat out at night, and if
repairs had to be done around the house, they were left for

Grace to do. After all, she was the one who built schoolhouses in Mexico.

Grace earned almost twice what Ron did because she really hustled, digging out the stories and following up leads other people dismissed. She produced good work, and she was proud of it. Ron, on the other hand, did no legwork or reporting. He read whatever copy his news director handed him, but exerted no effort, even at that. He sometimes mispronounced the names of important places, and other names he never attempted at all. By referring only to "the capital of Honduras," for instance, he could avoid trying to say "Tegucigalpa." In short, Ron was a first-class drone.

The drone sat beside her now, under the marquee, watching Beth Anne Warden's wedding reception unfold. Ron didn't like weddings, he claimed. They reminded him too much of his one mistake in life. Then he would snicker as if it were a joke. Grace didn't see it as one. And, she could tell that deep down, neither did he. He was drinking too much again today. The Wardens weren't serving liquor at this reception, so Ron had tanked up ahead of time.

How could she have missed all his glaring faults when they dated? Here she was, a seasoned reporter trained to observe, and that fluff-head had pulled the wool right over her eyes.

Grace watched her friend, the former Beth Anne Warden, dancing the first waltz with her groom, Alan. They looked so happy, so in love.

Beth Anne and Grace met and became fast friends through their sorority. Grace was an alumnae; Beth Anne was an active member. The two women hit it off instantly. Grace could see a lot of potential in Beth Anne. Grace became Beth Anne's mentor, offering valuable advice and making promising contacts for Beth Anne as Beth Anne entered the business world fresh from college.

Now, Grace remembered how animated Beth Anne was when she first told Grace about Alan.

"You'd like him, Grace," Beth Anne exclaimed. "He's a real cowboy. And sooooo good-looking!"

Grace watched the happy couple dance across the floor. She had tried to warn her friend about marriage—its pitfalls and false promises. But, Beth Anne's head was in the clouds from the first moment she met Alan.

Boy, Beth Anne, she thought, *you just wait!*

Everyone's marriage, like Grace's—yes, and Beth Anne's, too —changes with time. So often, the changes are not for the better.

Who's Sorry Now?

Our very nature throws into marriage certain clinkers that we do not recognize and cannot anticipate. Our families-of-origin generated those clinkers by the way our relatives did things, said things, and hid things. Dr. Robert Hemfelt likens them to time-release capsules.

Remember the twelve-hour cold capsule? It contained hundreds of tiny beads of medication. As your stomach digested the capsule, these beads would lie waiting to kick into action throughout the day to relieve your cold symptoms. You had to take only one capsule to gain a day's worth of relief. And all the medication wouldn't hit you at once like a Mack truck. Slowly over the day, the medication would trickle into your system relieving your runny nose, scratchy eyes, sore throat, and head congestion. A wonderful invention—at least, so said the inventors.

The time-release capsules Dr. Hemfelt speaks of may not be as wonderful. Things can be chugging along comfortably in your relationship. Suddenly, with no warning, one of those time-release beads is set off. The union is not what it was, and something has gone dreadfully awry.

Yet these clinkers, and the other inevitable changes in a marriage, can be turned from bad to good once you recognize what they are. Grace's marriage appeared dull and mundane to her; there are ways she and Ron could make it sparkle. We will discuss them. A hopeless situation can emerge into bright promise. A good union can be made better. It all depends upon finding and managing the sources of trouble, the clinkers, and changes. We want to help you do that.

Hints of Trouble

Couples who approach professionals in our clinic rarely come in because everything is going well. Rather, they sense trouble. They sense unmet needs. Their symptoms, the surface clues to underlying problems, show up in our case files again and again, however unique the problems may seem to the couples experiencing them. Because no marriage is perfect, every couple weathers these problems to some extent. But when the problems loom too large to handle and threaten the union, trouble will follow.

Look over the following hints of trouble in light of your own family relationships. Do some of them mar your happiness right now?

Chronic Financial Distress

Grace and Ron are DINKs—that's Double Income, No Kids. And yet, they simply cannot get ahead of their credit cards. Their savings account petered out a year ago. In this stage of life, prior to kids, they ought to be salting away all of Ron's paycheck, or perhaps his and part of hers. But the money seems to simply evaporate and Grace can't understand why.

Not all financial distress points to marriage problems, of course. We do, however, consider chronic financial difficulties a factor to look at closely. We also look closely if a person experiences constant or recurring vocational failure. This often points to some individual psychological problem or anger in the marriage. Ron and Grace will have to find these issues and work through them before they can establish a good relationship. Once a solid relationship is in place, they will be able to tackle their financial issues.

In-law Problems and Involvement

A related financial clue we address is any monetary dependence of the married couple upon the in-laws.

"But they prepared for us with trusts and legacies!" the couple might protest.

"Absolutely. And we're all in favor of it. Inheritances as frosting on the cake are marvelous. What we look for, rather, is the prospect that the couple requires that legacy in order to survive financially."

Far more telling is a situation in which the in-laws provide financial or intense emotional support long beyond the wedding, after the couple should have cut the economic and emotional apron strings and become independent.

In fact, in-law problems in general suggest that unfinished business—yearnings and conflicts that were never resolved—lie in the background. And though we will discuss unfinished business in detail later, keep in mind for now this broad generalization: Severe in-law friction indicates a cross-generational problem that, if not resolved, will fester in the present generation and infect the next one.

Family Imbalance and Stress

Grace grew up in a them-and-us family. She had one sister and two brothers. Her parents fought a lot, and when they fought, they would jockey furiously to line the kids up on the winning side. Grace usually found herself siding with Mom against Dad and her brothers. The fight would end when Mom slammed the bedroom door and bolted it from the inside.

When Uncle Ernie was involved, and he usually was, the kids would side with him and the parents would take the other side of the fence. Grace hated this, but she recognized that it was necessary. When you're fending for yourself in a family of six-plus-Uncle-Ernie, you need allies or the sharks will eat you.

In one fell swoop, Grace's family of origin illustrates what we look for in family imbalances: chronic fighting, sexual dysfunction, factional alliances ("them" against "us"), and problems with and about kids.

Emotional or Psychological Dysfunctions

Jocelyn, a former model, fought chronic depression for three years. Her husband sympathized, but he couldn't really understand her attitude. After all, he wasn't depressed. Their marriage was fine, their economic situation stable, the in-laws a thousand miles away. Obviously, he pointed out, it was her problem. Only when he entered into counseling with her and changed some basic attitudes and behaviors did her problem disappear.

During counseling, Jocelyn's husband found that he behaved a certain way in his marriage based upon his upbringing. His father invoked the stereotypical macho-male image—he never showed affection or emotion towards his wife or kids. Jocelyn's husband learned that behavior from an early age. He stopped being demonstrative towards Jocelyn once courtship and the newlywed years faded away. His example of how a man should act in a family was, of course, his father. Only when he was able to recognize this childhood conditioning and display more of his feelings to Jocelyn, was Jocelyn able to emerge from her depression.

Any emotional or psychological difficulty in one marital partner will invariably influence, and be influenced by, the other partner. Always.

Other symptoms we look for are anxiety, chemical dependence and addictions, and driving compulsions such as extreme perfectionism, workaholism, spendaholism, and such. Threats of suicide obviously hoist huge red banners.

What About You?

"Nothing wrong with my marriage!" you boast. Good for you! Perhaps none of the above hints of trouble apply to you. Would your spouse agree? Pause a moment and go through our list again. Check those topics that apply to your marriage as you see it. Add more if you can think of any:

_____ Chronic Financial Distress
_____ In-law Problems and Involvement
_____ Family Imbalance and Stress
_____ Emotional or Psychological Dysfunctions

_____ _____

_____ _____

If you checked any of these signs of trouble, your marriage may need some help. How about your spouse? How would he or she view each trouble sign? Has your spouse ever complained or nagged about one of these topics? Has your spouse ever seemed to go overboard with symptoms of compulsion or depression? If so, you may have a problem you didn't know about. It's worth considering.

The Influence of the Passages

"Many of the problems couples will face in later years," says Dr. Robert Hemfelt, "don't show up in premarital dating."

And let's face it: a good portion of what the person planning marriage experiences in premarital dating doesn't sink in. During early marriage, both partners are literally blinded by love, as Grace had been and as Beth Anne was. But then a hard, heavy dose of reality knocks the partners up alongside the head, and they both seem to change before each other's eyes. The kids multiply the chaos. And those time-release capsules, the hidden agendas, start popping. After a few years of marriage, the couple can almost always use some help. And that's what this book is about.

The symptoms of trouble we mentioned before will steal the sheer pleasure of marriage and are best scrubbed right now, before they become deeply ingrained. But they are merely the surface fluff. Their presence in your marriage, and their presence in the couples we counsel, say that something far deeper is going on. In this book we want to plumb the depths and sources of problems, rather than bandage the surfaces. These depths, the inner workings of marriage, can be compared to the dynamics of a softball game, believe it or not.

(Note: If you have read our first book in this series *New Love,* the rest of this chapter and the next will be a review. You may want to skip ahead to Chapter Three. However, if you are not familiar with the First Passage or other Passages of Marriage, we invite you to continue reading. Also, since many readers may only read the book in this series of five passages that applies to their immediate passage, we have repeated certain key concepts such as how to address anger, conflict, and sexuality in more than one book. If you have read more than one book in this series you may encounter repetition. However, we urge you to be open to the possibility that these subjects are so vital that they bear such repetition.)

The Dynamics of Marriage

The city league softball player steps up to the plate, shoulders his bat, and watches intently. Here comes the pitch . . . "It's a solid hit into deep right field!" the announcer screams exuberantly. The ball is still airborne as the player rounds first. It drops into tall grass—*very* deep right field—and a portly fielder scurries after it. The player passes third, homeward bound.

Wait! He failed to touch second! As his team groans in unison, he runs back to stomp second base. What would have been a home run ends up only a double, all because the runner failed to clear second base satisfactorily. Marriage is like that. We call the bases "passages."

When Doctors Newmans or Minirth or Hemfelt deal with the marital problems of couples in their counsel, they deal with three entities: the husband, the wife, and the marriage itself, as if the marriage were a living, breathing organism. We have found that if a marriage is not growing, it is dying, just as you would say for any living organism. When a marriage gets hung up in a passage, it ceases growing. Growth is, therefore, critical.

By definition, then, *passages are predictable and necessary stages, involving the physical, the emotional, and the spiritual dimensions of the union.* Through them, partners journey toward the lifetime goal of growth as individuals and as a couple.

In our personal lives and in our professional practice, the six authors of this book have identified five distinct stages, passages through which marriage passes. The developmental stages through which a child passes from birth into adulthood are well known. Similarly, a marriage matures from developmental stage to stage—from passage to passage—according to the number of years it has existed. Remarriage may differ somewhat; because the partners have been married previously, they might telescope a passage into a briefer time or extend a passage beyond its normal life span.

The Passages of Marriage

Not counting courtship, which by definition is a passage of premarriage, we divide the lifetime of a married couple into five discrete units. Although some people hasten ahead of time into the next passage, or linger a little longer than average in one passage or another, in general, healthy marriages hew pretty close to this outline. The passages are these:

- The First Passage—New Love, the first two years / Whether the couple be eighteen years old or eighty, they pass first through this dewy-eyed stage of idealized love. Persons who have been married previously may go through it a little faster than those married for the first time, but everyone tastes its heady joy.
- The Second Passage—Realistic Love, from the second anniversary through the tenth / Kids and career put the push on. About now, too, a heavy dose of reality sets in. This perfect partner is not so perfect after all. If this is Eden, why the thorns?
- The Third Passage—Steadfast Love, from the tenth anniversary through the twenty-fifth / Wrapped up in career, kids, and a host of extraneous, time-consuming activities, the couple find themselves fallen into a rut. Either they're mushing along complacently or at each other's throats, but there's a predictability about the whole thing.
- The Fourth Passage—Renewing Love, from the twenty-fifth anniversary through the thirty-fifth / As the kids fledge and the career peaks out, the meaning and purpose of life alters forever. Now what?
- The Fifth Passage—Transcendent Love, more than thirty-five years of marriage / What a history this couple has! The texture of the marriage changes as the couple enter retirement and watch youth fade for forever.

As the marriage moves from one of these passages to another —from base to base toward home plate, if you will—it also moves through specific conditions common to the human race. Crisis and conflict, intimacy, forgiveness, children, and memories form some of them.

Each of the passages through which every married couple travel, like bases on a softball diamond, must be appropriately dealt with if the next one is to count. And the tasks that accompany these passages must be completed before the next tasks commence. By tasks we mean attitude changes one must make and jobs one must complete in order to maintain an intimate marital relationship.

Should a runner skip over a base, inadvertently or on purpose, dire problems result. Should a runner get stuck on one base, the only way he can leave is by walking away scoreless. That's infinitely less satisfying than making it to home plate, for the aim of the game from the very beginning is to make it home.

Carl and Bess Warden, grandparents of the bride Beth Anne, married forty-eight years, were making it home. As painful as eventual separation and death would be, the Wardens both would know the peace and satisfaction of being able to say, "We did it."

One of every two married couples will never know that satisfaction.

During their long life together, Carl and Bess did not talk to marriage counselors or become involved in marriage therapy of any sort, though counsel might have helped them navigate the difficult passages more easily. Yet Carl and Bess did not simply muddle through. They worked diligently at their marriage, and to the very end enjoyed the fruits of a growing, timeless, abiding love.

You may be thinking, "But my marriage is so different; nobody has a husband like mine, or a wife like mine."

Don't be so sure.

What If My Marriage Doesn't Fit the Pattern?

Remember the age-guessing booth at fairs and carnivals long past? A rather rough-looking man with a four-day stubble would offer to guess your age within three years. If he guessed, he won and you paid him. If he missed, you won and he paid you. And he almost always won. Why? Because age makes itself known in certain ways, and the trained eye can see those ways in every person.

A marriage also ages in certain ways regardless of the persons involved, regardless of the circumstances. The same patterns prevail even though yours may be a most unusual union. In fact, what is "normal"?

Mary Alice and Frank Minirth know their marriage could probably never be considered normal. "When we married, we were both in school," Mary Alice explains. "Frank, in medical school, studied day and night. I had two years yet to complete my degree, so I was studying too. It wasn't a normal start-a-family situation.

"My first job was as a teacher in inner-city Little Rock, Arkansas. Definitely not normal! Frank worked twenty-five-hour days completing his internship. Then, getting a practice started —not normal. Possibly, there's no such thing as a normal marriage."

Your own situation may be less stressful than the Minirths', or it could be more stressful. You may be fishing off the Alaskan coast or working in a bank in Topeka. What's normal?

The passages themselves are the norm, the common denominators of any marriage. They are universal. They form the skeleton upon which problems and pleasures attach.

Each of the authors of this book is at a different passage: Brian and Debi Newman in the Second Passage, Robert and Susan Hemfelt just approaching the Third Passage, and Frank and Mary Alice Minirth in the Fourth. All six of us will share with you our personal experiences. We who are therapists will share our professional insights. In addition to counseling couples and leading marriage enrichment seminars, psychotherapists Brian and Debi put their advanced degrees to work on the staff of the Minirth-Meier Clinic. Dr. Minirth, psychiatrist and cofounder of the clinic, takes special interest in marriage and family dynamics. Dr. Robert Hemfelt, psychologist, is well known and respected as a leader in the study of codependency and multigenerational issues.

This Book: The Second Passage

This book deals with the Second Passage, from about the third year of marriage through, say, ten years. It incorporates all the material on the Second Passage that is covered in our hardcover book *Passages of Marriage* (Thomas Nelson, 1991).

In addition, you will find material and details we simply had no room for in our hardcover when we were discussing the problems and opportunities a lifelong marriage offers.

If your first marriage ended in divorce, it is important for your future happiness that you see the underlying reasons why it failed. We may be able to help you with that. At the bottom of most divorces, trouble came when one or both partners got hung up in a passage and failed to complete its tasks.

We will suggest ways to avoid fruitless friction and damaging conflict, and even how to turn conflict into a positive experience. Then, we will look at the tremendous payoff of a good marriage you keep patched up and treated right.

Before you get too far into the examination of your Second Passage of marriage, it will help to review the way the First Passage operated. Let's do that first.

Chapter 2

Have You Successfully Completed the First Passage?

C arl Warden hated to see a grown man cry, himself least of all. But the tears ran freely down his cheeks now, as Beth Anne came down the aisle. Praise God, she was beautiful! Warm, clear, suntanned skin against the white gown; long golden hair like her grandmother's, tumbling in loose waves; that uncertain, innocent smile. She was almost as beautiful as his Bess had looked. Beside him, Bess gripped his arm and squeezed.

He thought about his own wedding nearly half a century ago. Curious. He could no longer remember the feelings of first love exactly, though he could remember clearly how intense those feelings were. The love had changed drastically with the years. The intensity had not.

The wedding went off without a hitch and, for the first time in his life, Carl found himself stepping into a limo, a white stretch that needed two zip codes to park in.

Bess wagged her head "Can you imagine this?" Carefully she lowered herself in the seat. "When we got married we didn't ride around in limos."

"Naw." Carl chuckled and settled in beside her. "But as I recall, our wedding vehicle cost more than this does."

She laughed out loud. "True. A city bus costs more!"

At the reception, Carl shook hands with more people in two

hours than he'd met in the last three years. Louis Ajanian, a friend of his, was there with his new wife Marj. To look at Louis now you wouldn't have guessed barely a year ago this man was in the depths of depression over his first wife's death. Today Louis was as exuberant as a puppy dog. Carl smiled. "Love conquers all," he mused.

Among the people Carl met was the news anchor of a small independent TV station. Carl had seen the man on television a few times. It was his wife, though, who intrigued Carl. Grace Chevington was such a striking woman, beautiful and witty, the kind of lady Beth Anne seemed to gravitate toward.

"I think I've figured out why we always cry at weddings," said Grace toward the end of the afternoon.

"We're touched by beauty?" Carl suggested.

"Touched by sadness. You see this beautiful love in bloom, and you know it can't last."

Carl mulled that over a moment. He looked at her face, a very pretty face with very little happiness in it. "I feel so sorry for you," he thought.

Carl also met Julia Karris at last. Beth Anne had been talking about her good friend Julia for years. Beth had described Julia's woes with the ex-husband, the present husband, the kids and the step-kids. Too bad about all the problems. Julia was such a charming woman, graceful, dark-haired, and beautiful.

Everyone, like Grace, like Julia, and like Carl and Bess, sees the marriage union change with time. It can grow in beauty, or it can shrivel and die. The place to start directing those inevitable changes is at the very beginning.

The First Passage

A lifetime. In the blur of a breathless moment, the wedding day comes and goes. The lifetime stretches out before the happy couple. The First Passage forms the foundation of this lifetime commitment.

Let us briefly review the tasks that must be met for this First Passage to be satisfactorily completed.

The First Task: To Mold into One Family

The first task newlyweds must accomplish if they are to complete the First Passage—to mold two absolutely different, independent persons into one unit—doesn't come easily. It didn't come easily for Carl and Bess Warden two generations ago. Grace and Ron haven't completed that task yet. Beth Anne and Alan will also find some rough sledding.

Unity vs. Individuality

Take two headstrong individuals and forge them into a unit without sacrificing their individuality. What a formidable task! Several things help.

A powerful tool comes built in: excitement and enthusiasm. Raw, exuberant energy. On the other hand, one thing seriously hinders the move to unity: the possibility of breakage.

"Breakage?" exclaims the new couple. "What could break? We're young and indestructible and in love."

Regardless of what the couple think (or imagine), their intimacy in the beginning is superficial. True intimacy grows only as a couple get to know each other better. Persons in a new relationship have not had enough chronological time to do that in depth. They feel compelled to walk on eggs, as it were, when dealing with each other. "Will this upset her?" "How will I tell him about _____?" Much as they like to think they are deeply united, they are still individuals thinking in individual ways. Time can deepen the level of intimacy, secure the bond. Unfortunately, many marriages end in these first years, during this tenuous period.

Expecting More of the Marriage Than It Can Provide

Those time-release capsules Dr. Hemfelt mentioned in Chapter 1 can create a barrier to growth and intimacy. One or both partners may call upon this new union to heal prior relationships with parents and other relatives. We will discuss them at length as a Second Passage issue.

Pulling Up Roots

Pulling up roots exists in many dimensions. The bride and groom have successfully left home. They're on their own. But the home has not left them.

The old patterns from home color nearly everything in the new marriage. Do you open gifts on Christmas Eve or Christmas morning? Do you make your bed immediately upon rising or when you go through the house tidying up? Which is right? The way you did it when you were growing up is right, of course. Any other way, though not exactly wrong, isn't right, however.

Think for a moment of your own marriage. How much of your mate's petty idiosyncracies are founded on the way *you* were raised? The question is worth considering in depth and at leisure. You can "cure" a mate's annoying habits by either changing the habits or changing your annoyed response. Identifying the source of the annoyance often ameliorates it.

One of the places where we often find family roots causing problems is in money matters.

Getting a Hold on the Money

Who will handle the finances in the new family? Individuals accustomed to financial autonomy will have severe adjustments to make, if money and the decisions surrounding it are to become family matters.

Do we adhere to a budget?

Who balances the checkbook and reconciles the bank statements?

Who does the income tax?

Who has the final say on major purchases?

These and similar questions reveal not only a couple's divergent views of money but also in what ways they diverge. It is one thing to know you disagree with your spouse; it is much more helpful to know exactly where and how much you disagree.

Susan Hemfelt remembers a particular incident early in their marriage. "Robert and I considered buying a hot tub. He wanted one so badly. I thought it was impractical when we needed other things for the house. The more he pleaded his case, the more I thought a hot tub was a 'luxury' and not a 'necessity.' We 'needed' furniture that blended together as well as coordinating curtains and rugs.

"After we mulled the issue over and over, a new thought occurred to me: We did have enough furniture and curtains to get by, so maybe in Robert's eyes, these purchases were 'luxuries' also. Then I remembered where we first met and his need for some form of relaxation. I decided to change my position on the matter.

"Also, I decided (*and this is the key*) this was not a crucial issue that I had to win. We got the hot tub. Later the new furniture and curtains for the house came along."

She grins. "Wouldn't you know it, we had different preferences (and still do) for the temperature of the water. Many times I threatened to invite the neighborhood over for a shrimp boil in our hot tub that Robert keeps so hot! But, it's his toy. I relinquished control on this one."

How About You?

How about you and your spouse? What issues really matter to you? What issues are critical for your mate? Discuss them. These issues should be resolved as part of the First Passage's completion.

We often suggest that a couple enter into a financial covenant with one another, no matter what passage of marriage they may be in. Are you and your spouse willing to establish a covenant, which will help eliminate any ghosts from your past? Consider a verbal or written agreement like the one below:

- "I agree that money will never be more important than our relationship."
- "I agree to let you know if I think that either of us is becoming irresponsible about financial matters."
- "I agree to stay within the budget we plan together."
- "I agree that from our wedding on, money is ours and the problems and joys it brings are also ours to share."
- "I agree that credit cards can be a major problem, so I'll always talk to you before making a purchase over $_____."

- "I agree to work with you until we agree on how to pay, and who will pay, the bills in our marriage."

Saying Good-bye

Part of pulling up those old family roots is saying good-bye to the pain of your childhood.

Pain from Your Childhood Family

Other books, such as *Love Is a Choice: Recovery for Codependent Relationships* by Dr. Robert Hemfelt, Dr. Frank Minirth, and Dr. Paul Meier (Nashville: Thomas Nelson, Inc., 1989), deal at length with a curious phenomenon Minirth-Meier counselors see constantly. That is, the more dysfunctional and unsatisfying a child's family of origin has been, the harder it is for the child to leave it. Logic suggests that if the original family failed to serve that person's needs, leaving home is the solution. But human beings do not operate on logic. A majority of our decisions may be made below the conscious level, in the deep recesses of thought and sub-thought where logic does not apply.

We frequently find adult children who have remained over-involved with their parents. Frequently, too, the parents become so enmeshed in their children that they are loathe to give them up. Such was the case of a newlywed named Marla. Her father died when she was nine. As she matured, an only child, she and her mother descended into a frenetic love-hate relationship.

Marla married to get away, but not very far away. She and her husband lived across town. Marla's mother felt free to pop in on them any time, for any reason, or for no reason at all. "Oh, don't bother," she would say as she barged in. "It's only me." Unfortunately, Marla had become so codependently involved with Mom that she didn't realize how badly Mom was overstepping and destroying their personal boundaries.

Wearied beyond patience by this invasion of his privacy, her husband found a job in Minneapolis and summarily carted Marla off a thousand miles from her mommy. Six months later the widow retired. To Minnesota.

Leaving home residentially is more than a step forward in individualization. It is also an important step toward learning to love. When we initially assess patients in the clinic, one of the things we look for at first is whether the adult client has left home residentially, financially, and in other ways.

Some of those other ways a client should have left home are socially, vocationally and avocationally, and in the realm of civic identity—that is, who am I in the community?

Beth Anne, for example, joined a sorority. Neither of her parents were Greeks. She starred in high school and college volleyball. Her mom claimed to be a klutz at anything athletic, and her father was more into intellectual pursuits—a member of the chess team, not sports teams. Beth Anne majored in business because she wanted to do the same sort of thing her mom did—not because she wanted to follow in mom's footsteps, but because she had seen her mom's job from the inside, so to speak, and she liked it.

Thus, Beth Anne followed her parents' paths in some regards and departed from their paths in others. The important thing was, she was beginning to listen to her own drummer.

What this all comes to, you see, is a solid sense of self. The more secure the sense of self, the more ready that person is for love. Persons who fail to emerge as independent entities in this important First Passage of marriage will try to find and complete their identities through the identities of their mates. And that, the heart of codependency problems, makes for an unhealthy and unstable marital relationship.

Once the couple has successfully uprooted from their original families, attention shifts to. . .

The New Family

Marla in Minnesota had to become a tightrope walker. You've seen the high-wire balancing acts at the circus. Some of them feature a comic performer, a person who, although highly skilled, pretends to be a novice. As he steps out onto the wire he wobbles crazily; the crowd giggles. He "falls," bouncing on the wire; the crowd gasps. He extends his arms and waves them up and down, lurching back and forth. The crowd waits for the inevitable fall.

The audience understands this parody of proper balance because a novice would do exactly those things—wobble precariously, flail wildly, fail to find their center of balance, move in fits and jerks rather than smoothly. Novices in marriage also do those things as they seek a comfortable balance between all their new and altered relationships.

In shifting to their new family, and in putting original family patterns behind, the couple in the first flush of new love must completely reshape all their other relationships. Finding the new balance point is inevitably rocky. You've never seen such wild flailing and tilting! They have to bring new balance to:

Relationships with the Family-of-Origin

A traditional Navajo husband will never look at his mother-in-law or speak to her. Even when driving her to town, he'll stay in the cab of his pick-up while she sits in the back, riding the fifty or so miles in the open air.

Think also of all those stale Henny Youngman mother-in-law jokes. In-law conflicts and adjustments, though, are far more delicate, and can be far more rewarding, than the jokes and customs suggest.

Here you are in a whole new family, all of whose members know your spouse better than you do. They fit together like an old shoe; you feel like a cellist in a drum and bugle corps. There is no formula for adjusting to the in-laws. Each case is individual, each situation unique. That makes finding balance all the harder. The balance becomes nearly impossible until both newlyweds successfully pull up roots from the old home.

To all these tugs between the couple and the in-laws, you can add the new relationship with siblings. Brothers and sisters are no longer the main same-generation support people. And yet, their roles, though changed drastically, should not diminish. More balancing.

Then there are the many other relationships that you had before you were married; they, too, will change.

Relationships with Single Friends

She still wants to run around with her girlfriends, shopping perhaps or just doing what they used to do together, and for the best of reasons: These are her friends. He yearns for his boys' night out with old, familiar buddies, where guys can be themselves in all their take-me-as-I-am glory.

And how about a foursome or party? It used to be, the guests had to be compatible with only the host or hostess. Now the guests have to be compatible with the couple. In a foursome, he and she both have to mesh satisfactorily with she and he. It isn't easy. Finding other couples who fit well as a group becomes quite a complex process, with lots of false starts and disappointments.

Speaking of singles, both partners must say good-bye to past romantic relationships and dreams. The infamous bachelor party symbolizes the joking but not-so-joking "This is your last fling, pal" end of an era. Raucous as such parties are, they are also sad. The groom-to-be rightfully grieves his loss of the past, even as he rejoices in the many advantages his future promises.

One of the big losses of his past, and hers too, is total control.

The Second Task: Deciding Who's in Control

Control is another of those pivotal issues in a new family. Who controls what and to what degree? These questions must be resolved over and over again throughout the marriage because couples' circumstances change constantly. What works well today may not work at all tomorrow. We will deal with control at length as a Second Passage issue. Be aware that it is the root of many problems in the First Passage as well.

The Third Task: Building a Sexual Union

"Doin' What Comes Natchurly" was a popular song of a generation ago. It suggests that all you have to do to enjoy marital bliss is follow your natural inclinations. Not so. Letting nature take its course would be sufficient, were sex primarily biological. It is not. Unlike other biological needs—food, shelter, water—the sex drive is profoundly influenced by factors outside biology. Physical factors such as drugs or alcohol, fatigue, stress, and physical disabilities alter sexual response. But the most active sex organ, and the least appreciated, is the brain. It participates largely beyond the conscious level. Personal problems and distractions, fear, misconceptions about sex ("hang-ups," if you will), and the emotional states of both parties are subconscious mental factors.

Today, newlyweds come to bed armed with all sorts of "safe sex" information but with very little information about what really happens emotionally and physiologically. As part of the First Passage adjustments, they must deal with physiology and emotion. We will assume that by the Second Passage the couple has figured out more or less the physiological roles of man and woman. But emotional difficulties may still abound.

Newlyweds may suppress emotional problems in the heat of love, so to speak. That ardor cools somewhat by the Second Passage and the suppressed emotional difficulties surface. Also, hidden agendas start breaking forth more so in subsequent passages than in the first. These time-release beads, as well as sexual considerations themselves, are important enough that we will deal with them separately as Second Passage issues. Keep in mind that if their First-Passage versions haven't been dealt with, you'll be facing them now and they will loom even larger.

The Fourth Task: To Make Responsible Choices

Whatever could you have been thinking of! You've done a lot of rock climbing, scaling some spectacular rock faces. Then you let your friend talk you into climbing the Cap. How could you have been so crazy? Now here you are in Yosemite National Park, clinging to the sheer face of the granddaddy of all rocks, the monolithic El Capitan.

You left the loose talus at the base of the rock fifty feet below you and now you are climbing the vertical surface using only the handholds and footholds you find along the way. In a crack here you tuck your fingertips; you wrap your fingers around a hand-sized bulge there, very tightly. A patch where rock sloughed off left a one-inch-wide ledge. You set your toes firmly on that minuscule ledge and put your weight on it. You rise another foot and a half.

You have 3600 feet to go.

You planned your ascent from the ground, following with

eye and topographical map the exact route you would take up the face. But once on the face you cannot see the whole. You cannot even see ten feet above you most of the time. Despite that, you have no idea what lies ahead, for every foot of the way you must make decisions. They are crucial decisions; a wrong choice can put you in a position you cannot climb your way out of. You'd be stuck, unable to go either up or down. And once you commit yourself to a certain handhold and a certain direction, you have summarily cut yourself off from all the other advantages and disadvantages a slightly different direction would have offered. Of all the hundreds of different ways up El Cap, with your choices you instantly limit yourself to a very narrow corridor of possibilities.

Choices in marriage are exactly like that. You must make telling, sometimes irrevocable decisions about the future even though you cannot see ten feet, or ten minutes, into it. Certain such choices are common to nearly every marriage in its first two years. Some of them are:

The Urge to Run vs. Hanging Tough

A number of fears hit newlyweds between the eyes during the first few years of marriage:

- "What's the big deal about intimacy? You say that this or that leads to greater intimacy as if intimacy were a goal. Not to me, it's not. I want my space, and my wife can keep hers. Too much intimacy messes up a relationship."

That's fear talking. To be intimate is to be vulnerable. Many people, men and women alike, are afraid of that kind of vulnerability. Other fears are just as common. For instance the young married sometimes thinks:

- "I'm stuck. I just bought into one romantic partner for a lifetime. I just blew any chance to do better!"

Fear of entrapment is a frequent concern of our clients. Such fears bring divorce or abandonment to the minds of most newly marrieds sooner or later. Bailing out is definitely a dead-end solution, but in the face of fear it may look inviting. This also includes threatening to bail out ("That's it. No more. I'm going home to Mother.").

As Dr. Hemfelt points out, the urge to run has never been easier to indulge than in the twentieth century. "There are few —if any—moral, social, or even ethical stigmas attached to divorce. We've lost the powerful peer pressures that used to keep people married."

Bolt or stay? These are the two major choices, and there is no undoing the damage if you take the wrong route up the rock.

Resisting Change vs. Going with the Flow

Here is a major decision that pops up frequently in marriage: to adjust and compromise, or to resist change and pretend things are working.

A case in point: Gretchen and Tim Heusen. Gretchen and Tim both grew up in fairly affluent families. Eight months into their marriage, they were begging Daddy Heusen and Daddy Mullins to help them get their credit cards under control and co-sign for their house. Wisely, Daddies Heusen and Mullins conferred before addressing the newlyweds and discovered the couple's problem.

The fathers knew that newlyweds almost always take a big drop in their standard of living, and logically so. Their earning power is as yet nowhere near where it will be someday, their total assets negligible because they've not had time to accumulate much. Gretchen and Tim, however, chose to pretend their circumstances had not changed. They could not adjust to the new reality and, as a result, had acquired heavy debts beyond their ability to pay.

Their story has a happy ending, though not an easy one. Daddies Heusen and Mullins sat down together with the kids, showed them how to consolidate debts, and offered advice on how to live more economically (both dads knew a trick or two in that department; both had started with nothing). The couple was smart enough to listen to their fathers' counsel. Six months later, when Gretchen and Tim showed they were adjusting to their situation by making good progress at paying off their debts, their fathers bought the house themselves. Today, they rent it to the kids as an income property. When Gretchen and Tim have built up enough savings for a down payment, they'll be able to buy the house.

In this case the climbers, Gretchen and Tim, started out along one route, realized it was the wrong one, and were able to head up in a new and better direction. The Heusens were able to adjust their lifestyle expectations.

Many couples are not so wise. In our times, most people try to start their marriage at the same economic level as their parents—not realizing that it took their parents years to obtain that financial status. Susan Hemfelt's parents began with just a card table and boxes for furniture. Today's newly marrieds can't conceive doing this.

For instance, Mark Brown was an accountant, making $25,000 to $28,000 a year. Jessica, his wife, came from a wealthy family. The first year of their marriage, she went wild with the charge cards, going to department stores every chance she got. She was still living at her parents' economic level. Both Mark and Jessica wound up in our counsel when their finances were a disaster and all communication between them had broken down.

"Didn't you both sit down and plan a budget?" we asked Mark alone.

"Sure. But Jes just looked at the budget. She wouldn't stick to it—she still bought everything in sight."

Jessica Brown had not adjusted to her new lifestyle. Her expectations remained high even on Mark's moderate salary. Their story also has a happy ending. Although Mark was up to his ears in debt from Jessica's spending habits, he didn't want a divorce. He stuck with her and led the way in reducing spending. Jes finally came to grips with the fact she must defer some of her wants, sometimes indefinitely. She accepted her husband's financial leadership. As a result, she learned to improvise, to decorate and live well without spending money. Disguising beat-up furniture with perky slipcovers, buying judiciously from the thrift stores, and learning crafts to make instead of buy became a game. Mark and Jes adjusted their expectations of each other and their lifestyle.

Mary Alice Minirth talks about another aspect of adjusting. "Throughout our marriage, Frank and I have been careful to keep time just for each other. It has not been easy. A lot of times we've had to improvise—to be flexible. For instance, during his years of internship and getting started in practice, the kids and I would go over to the hospital to eat supper with him. It was the only break he had at a reasonable hour. Today, we may go out for breakfast before he does his radio show. Spur-of-the-moment things like that keep the romance alive and well. You have to roll with the punches; you have to be ready to improvise."

A third way newly marrieds find themselves forced to choose between flexibility and resisting change is when the newness starts to wear off. People in courtship try to keep their best foot forward. Still somewhat uncertain about their relationship, newlyweds maintain their best behavior, just as they did in courtship. Rarely does this best behavior last. Both partners must be ready to adjust to surprises as the real spouse emerges bit by bit.

Consider again the case of Mark and Jessica Brown. Jessica fondly envisioned Mark as a breadwinner making any amount she needed. After all, Daddy did. Mark assumed he had married a lady like Mom, who knew the value of a dollar and spent frugally. These attitudes, of course, arose in courtship. Mark and Jessica were seeing only what they wanted to see of each other, not reality.

After time passed, their façades wore off. Mark and Jessica began to see each other's true person—a rude awakening. Their challenge now was to adjust to living with these new and sometimes disappointing personalities.

This adjustment was difficult, which is why many couples bail out at this point. Couples that endure find enormous freedom when they no longer have to keep up a front to attract their mates. Each partner can now be truly themselves still loved by their spouses. In the best of circumstances, this love will mature.

How About You?

What adjustments did, or does, your particular situation require? How comfortable are you, or were you, at accepting those adjustments?

The last task of the First Passage of marriage deals with the passages of marriage themselves. Sooner or later, you and your spouse must recognize and analyze your parents' incompleted passages or these unresolved issues will join those other ghosts that may haunt your relationship.

The Fifth Task: To Deal with Your Parents'

Incomplete Passages

We have some good news and some bad news for you. The bad news: All the unresolved issues of your families' prior generations, those time-release beads that have been accumulating through the years, will affect you. These time-release beads are different from mere attitudes or methods of family life. These issues can be destructive to your relationship. Yet they often are so deeply buried beneath your conscious mind that you cannot tell they are there, nor can you escape them.

The good news: Although your ancestors failed to work out all their issues in the past, usually because they didn't realize they were there, you can overcome them. Recognizing the issues foisted upon you by prior generations is half the battle. Over and over, our patients and clients tell us how very liberating it feels as they recognize what is happening in their lives.

Prior generations may leave many kinds of unfinished business for us and our children to mop up—or suffer through. Not all unfinished business consists of incomplete marital passages. Unfinished business is anything the parents started and did not complete; dreams they entertained but did not fulfill; elements of life such as the opposite sex or fractured personal relationships with which they never made peace. The bottom line is: *All incomplete passages from one generation become unfinished business for the next.*

The next generation then must complete unfinished business or it will plague the generation still to come. If you inherited your parents' legacy of unfinished business, you condemn your children to suffer with, or to resolve the unfinished business you do not handle now. There is no easy way out.

These "ghosts" from your family of origin will haunt your marriage through all its passages. For this reason, dealing with the multigenerational issues will be a major task of most passages. Our past—our forebears, our childhood, our family of origin, our previous traumas—is sometimes expressed in a set of symbolic statements. The vow, "I do" in a marriage ceremony is one such statement. As we step up to the altar to speak our "I do's" before God and the world, our hearts speak one or more of the following "I do's" nonverbally.

1. "I DO attribute to you, my new partner, all of the unresolved negative gender stereotypes propagated by my mother and father."

By "propagated" we mean set forth by the parents. Grandparents, aunts, and uncles qualify here too. Negative stereotypes such as "No man can be trusted; they'll all stray from you"; "Women have no skill at managing money"; and "Men can't be expected to have sensitive feelings" may all spill over into the marriage.

We recall one couple, Shawna and Sam, in their First Passage of marriage who, during courtship, were absolutely eloquent in their words of endearment, commitment, and affection to one another. Shortly after the honeymoon, Shawna began to notice that, although Sam still displayed interest and affection, he never said "I love you." Gone were his impassioned declarations. When she drew it from him in a passive way: "Do you love me?" he would say yes. It ended there.

In the rural region where Sam grew up, men didn't express affection; that wasn't manly. His dad took it a step further. He delighted in teasing Mom and would never say words of affection for her in front of the kids. The only relationship displayed in front of the kids was derogatory. "How's the old bag today?" The obvious message Sam received was: husbands cannot be tender or endearing.

Interestingly, Shawna came to the hospital for tests. She suffered vaginal pain with no discernible physical cause. Doctors referred her for psychological counseling. Shawna was hurt and angry that her supposedly loving husband would not speak his love. The vaginal pain became an expression of her anger and hurt. Once both of them figured out what the problem was, the dysfunction was resolved. Now Sam knows it's okay to be tender and endearing in marriage as well as in courtship. And when he starts to slip into the old stereotypical patterns, she's quick to put him back on track.

2. *"I DO set about to continue the battle of the sexes unresolved between my mother and father. I DO carry the banner for my mother or father by reenacting the unfinished battle."*

"I see, now," said another patient we'll call Jerry. "If I had married a tender love-kitten, instead of Stone-Cold Molly, I wouldn't have been able to keep up the fight." The unresolved battle of the sexes between his mom and dad continued clear through Jerry's extended family. Aunts and uncles, cousins, siblings, all harbored resentments and hostilities against the opposite sex. "It all started back with that women's liberation thing," Grandpa grumped. "Things were okay 'til then." No, things weren't. Thanks to Grandpa, Jerry had inherited a battle generations old.

Because his father had a long-standing war to force his mother into sexual compliance and performance, Jerry subconsciously picked a frigid spouse. Jerry and his wife had two new battles to win. Jerry had to recognize that this battle was his dad's all along and Jerry had to hand it back to him; Jerry had to make new decisions for himself. The second battle was his wife's. She had shut down internally—sexually. Now she had to go back and explore why.

We suggest that you think about the fights between your parents. Be wary of that old nemesis denial, the natural response that causes us to minimize painful things in order to survive in a family. Also realize that often we can't see the forest for the trees. Everything about our family is familiar and comfortable. This familiarity hinders our perception and then we don't see the fallacies in our parents' relationship. Be aware of those time-release capsules, your unfinished business, lying in wait, ready to kick in.

Clients of Brian and Debi Newman had such a capsule that colored their early conflicts. Debi explains, "Each time Kevin and Joan Davenport had an argument, Joan would leave the scene and lie down on the bed in their spare room. For her, it was a chance to cool off, to get away from the emotions of the moment. Kevin acted very threatened by this."

Brian continues, "When Kevin's mother and father had a disagreement, his mom left the room and retired to the guest room. It was the same when Kevin and his mom had an argument. Her leaving meant case closed, no more discussion. The issue was never brought up again. Kevin's mom got her way by withdrawing from the conflict. But the conflict never was resolved."

Therapists call this passive aggression. By not doing anything or operating with subtle innuendos, the persons are achieving what they want. They are winning by lying down, in essence. Passive aggression is common and very effective. We normally think of aggressive people as violent, strong, and dominant. An aggressive person can be just as dominant if they act quiet and meek. In Kevin's situation, the fact that his mother was ill a lot in his childhood, and many times convalesced in the spare bedroom, added to the power this action represented.

Brian adds, "When Joan left a dispute and went to the spare room, Kevin felt that same despair he experienced with his mother. He also felt threatened by Joan's actions, as if he were back again in his mom's house, never winning an argument and helpless to change the cycle."

"Joan didn't realize how much her actions affected Kevin," Debi says. "When we explored the issue with them both, Joan saw how upset Kevin was when she went to the spare room, just like his mother did.

"The complicating factor was that Joan had a legitimate need to withdraw from the incident and cool off so she could think clearly. It was only her method that was threatening. We talked them through the conflict resolution process, and through lots of understanding and patience, Kevin has come to accept Joan's need to cool off and leave the situation for a while. He was only able to do this, however, when Joan proved to him she was committed to resolving the issue. Joan did that by agreeing to meet with Kevin at a later time (specific time and place) to discuss the problem. She had to follow through several times to convince him."

Brian smiles as he remembers the case. "Joan also had to make her actions less threatening to Kevin—avoiding the trigger for his time-release capsule. Now, she tries not to use the spare bedroom as a place to cool off."

How About You?

Often the battle of the sexes will be fought on battlefronts that involve authority issues, financial matters, sexual intimacy, and time sharing. Look carefully at the bottom-line cause of friction between your parents. To help patients identify these issues we often suggest that they look at their parents' relationship in five different ways. One of the five will usually reveal a clue about the real issues behind the friction.

The Known Conflict

For instance, you might have heard your mom complain over and over again that Dad doesn't make enough money or Dad doesn't know how to manage the money he does make. That's the overt conflict. Think about the arguments between your parents and determine the known conflict:

"When my mom and dad argued, it was most frequently about _____."
They also argued about _____."

The Suspected Conflict

You may have never heard either of your parents talk about this issue or fight about it, but you have a hunch that this problem was there, just below the surface.

Or this suspected conflict may be an issue underlying the main conflict. For instance Mom might have continually complained that Dad was a poor breadwinner, but in reality Mom was a compulsive shopper. Dad never confronted her about it, so the real conflict between them was hidden.

"I suspect that an underlying conflict between my parents was _____."

Underlying Fears

Behind most conflict and most anger is fear. We always ask patients if their parents had any strong fears. For instance, Mom never acknowledged her fear of poverty, but she did talk about the Christmas when her only gifts were an orange and an apple and a new pair of shoes because her father was out of work during the Great Depression. Her underlying fear was "We will never have enough money to avoid some financial disaster. We are going to run out of money and lose all we do have."

"I suspect that my mom's underlying fear was
_____."
"I suspect that my dad's underlying fear was
_____."

Disappointments or Disillusionments

Now ask yourself, "Did either of my parents experience any great disappointments or disillusionments?"

For instance your mom may never have said so directly, but you came to realize that she doesn't see Dad as "Mr. Right." This doubles the ante for you, if you're a girl, as you try to find your own "Mr. Right." It also doubles the ante for your husband to always perform as "Mr. Right."

"I suspect that my mom has been disappointed or disillusioned by _____."
"I suspect that my dad has been disappointed or disillusioned by _____."

Finally, we suggest that you compare notes with other family members.

Input From The Extended Family

Sisters or brothers, aunts or uncles, grandparents. When we counsel patients, we often ask permission to talk to a relative in a special session or by telephone. One phenomenon in family relationships can be illustrated by that old story of three blindfolded people who tried to describe an elephant. One touched the tail and described a hairy ball; another held the ears and described long floppy wings; another felt the tusks and described a hard cylinder. Each person had a piece of the picture, but no one could give a complete description of that elephant. We all see our family of origin with that same narrow incomplete perspective.

We suggest that you fill in the missing pieces by talking to someone in your family. Play back the memories of your parents' disagreements together, then think about their actions. Any signs of war? It's your battle as well as your parents' unless you give it back to them.

Concerning Jerry's wife (alias Stone-Cold Molly), incidentally, she eventually found out she harbored massive guilt and anger about an abortion forced onto her by her parents. She thought she had put all that behind her, but stuffing it away is not healthy grieving. She still occasionally goes back to grieve what her parents did to her and her unborn child.

3. *"I DO seek a safety zone in this marriage by selecting a spouse who will not challenge or threaten the area of greatest apparent vulnerability in my parents' marriage."*

The power of this "I do" is so great that a person may over-select their mate, making an extremely "safe pick." For example, the daughter of an authoritarian, tyrannical father chose a totally lifeless, passive wimp as a safe pick for marriage. Everyone who met him said, "Huh? Why?" The reason, of course: That partner would not run roughshod over her life. She found, six months into her marriage, that he didn't even run smoothshod over her life. He didn't run at all. Within months she was bored mindless with this man, left without a spark of romance or sensuality. "It's like being married to a potted plant," she lamented.

Grace Chevington, as we will find out, was so empowered by this "I do" that she selected Ron Reynolds as her mate.

Give these three "I do's" a lot of thought. Discuss them together, and then listen to what each other says.

And if at any time you feel you are in over your head—that you have uncovered something too big and too ugly to handle —do seek professional help.

Have You Completed the First Passage?

Before we begin to discuss the Second Passage of marriage and its unique challenges and tasks, take a moment to measure the progress of your marriage with the following questionnaire. Feel free to xerox a copy for your spouse. These are the type of questions we ask a couple to see if they mastered the tasks of the First Passage. Check the statements if they apply to you:

1. _____ "I am willing to bend on issues that have popped up regarding the nitty-gritty of married life: who balances the checkbook, who does what cooking,

who scrubs the toilet. As evidence of this, I can cite
the following example:

_____"

2. _____ "We have reached agreement, or at least armistice,
on some major control issues. Two specific instances I can point to that demonstrate progress
are:
1)_____
2)_____"

3. _____ "I am willing to step out of my old family into this
new one. Evidence that I am maturing into the new
life as a marriage partner, or have done so, is:

_____
_____"

4. _____ "I can step out of denial and honestly recognize
that I have not come as far out of my family as I
would like to, as illustrated by this instance:

_____
_____"
"Three things I can do to reduce overly dependent
family ties are:
1)_____
2)_____
3)_____"

5. _____ "I am willing to open up into intimacy. One recent
instance in which I let myself be vulnerable to my
mate is:

_____"

"In this last week, my mate and I found time alone
together (other than in bed!) _____ times."

6. _____ "I can honestly claim that our sex life is open and
honest and enjoyable for both of us, more so than
in the beginning.
A way in which it is improving is:

_____"

7. _____ "Okay. So I am willing to admit that my romance with a perfect partner is an illusion. As evidence that this statement is true, I offer this incident or point to demonstrate that I have genuinely made peace with my partner's imperfections:

_____."

8. _____ "I am willing to pursue romance with my spouse anyway. Three instances lately in which my partner and I made a romantic gesture or pursued some romantic fantasy are:

1)_____

2)_____

3)_____."

Now look back over your answers and your spouse's. If either of you could not check at least six of these statements, your marriage may not have taken full advantage of the First Passage. We suggest reading our first book, *New Love,* in our series on the Passages of Marriage. It can provide insights for you and your spouse to help you accomplish the tasks and reap the benefits of this First Passage.

However, if you and your spouse could check most if not all of these statements, congratulate yourselves. You have accomplished the tasks of the First Passage successfully.

You are now ready for the Second Passage.

From La-La Land to the Real World

At about two years of marriage, the observant couple will notice a lot of changes in a marriage and not all of them will be good. Let us assume you have safely negotiated at least these first two years, the first few hundred feet of El Capitan. Lord willing, you have a long and exhilarating adventure yet before you. Let us delve now into the Second Passage of marriage.

Like the individual pitches you must accomplish to reach the top of El Capitan, so must you accomplish specific tasks to complete this Second Passage. Those tasks will be discussed in greater detail in the following chapters. But first, you will need

a map of your route to make it to the top. The Second Passage
route map is displayed on page 47. Once studying your route,
you can begin.

There's nowhere to go but up.

THE SECOND PASSAGE TASKS

TASK ONE: HANG ON TO LOVE AFTER REAL-
ITY STRIKES

TASK TWO: CHILDPROOF YOUR MARRIAGE

TASK THREE: RECOGNIZE THE HIDDEN CON-
TRACTS IN YOUR MARRIAGE

TASK FOUR: WRITE A NEW MARRIAGE CON-
TRACT

Chapter 3

What Happens
When Reality
Sinks In?

B eth Anne's good friend, Julia Karris sat in our waiting room with a pencil and a magazine she had purchased at the grocery store. Thoughtfully, she went down through one of those quizzes that promise to reveal to you whether you've got a man to fit your temperament.

Finished at last, she compared her responses with the answers in the box. Then she thumbed on back to the recipe pages, but her heart dwelt on that quiz. According to the magazine, her first husband, Rick, had been absolutely right for her.

Jerry, her second husband, was absolutely wrong.

Taking tests is fun, if no grade point average hangs in the balance. Julia had a problem, though—two, in fact. One, she took the test seriously, and two, she was stuck in this Second Passage of marriage, tussling with a mega-dose of realism.

Brian Newman smiles at the memory of another test: "Debi and I tried out a test once that was fun to take. It was supposed to measure your temperament and some other things. In doing so it rated us on extremes: depressed versus light-hearted, self-controlled versus compulsive—that kind of thing. You rate yourself and you rate each other."

Debi nods. "It was a revelation, all right. Brian and I took it while we were both still in school. Brian rated himself high in self-control and rated me impulsive. But I rated us just the opposite; I thought Brian was impulsive and I had the self-control. As we talked about it, we came to realize why we responded that way."

Brian goes on, explaining: "Debi takes a very casual, cavalier attitude toward housework. Impulsive is not too strong a word. She flits to the next job before she finishes the first one. If it doesn't get done that day, she doesn't care. That was the basis on which I was rating her."

Debi concludes: "But I rated myself according to my on-the-job performance. At work I'm well organized and disciplined. So I saw myself as self-controlled. Brian is very well organized and self-controlled at home, but I was responding to him according to his schoolwork. He hated some aspects of school. He'd put off papers and projects, neglect study, and then have to cram at the end. I considered that impulsive and never looked at his behavior in the home apart from his school career.

"We were answering the questions not about the whole person but about one certain sphere of that person."

A Gem of Many Facets

Everyone knows that human beings are gems of many facets. We operate in a multitude of dimensions; in some of them we shine, in some we don't. Hardly anyone, though, uses that knowledge to understand and adjust to others. Even if men and women were simple, one-dimensional cardboard characters, the kind you used to watch on fifties television, they would still have difficulty meshing together. People are infinitely complex, and that makes true intimacy infinitely harder, for there is no way any two persons can complement each other completely in every dimension.

And yet, our media have convinced us that persons who are truly in love can move through life together in perfect synchronization. There's that vacuous "Happily Ever After" promise again.

Can two people learn to walk together without tripping over each other? The first task of this Second Passage in marriage is simple and yet extraordinarily difficult: Hang on to love after reality strikes.

The First Task: Hang On to Love After Reality Strikes

A pervasive so-far-so-good feeling helps the couple to hang on to love after reality strikes. "We've made it to this point; we've the impetus to keep going." Lord willing, in those first few years, the young marrieds (and remember this young-married business applies as much to elderly newlyweds as to teens) have ironed out some of the issues causing rifts in their relationship.

Life is as active and hectic right now as it's ever going to be. There is a momentum, like a strong tidal current, washing the couple along from day to day. Of course, getting caught in a riptide is no fun. Busy-ness may also work to disadvantage in a marriage.

A lot of things other than busy-ness can mess up the smooth progress of this passage.

What Hinders Completion?

This marriage is no longer new. Yet, it has not developed a long history. There is great power in the ability of a common history to unite people, whether it be nations or a married couple. Add to that the fact that couples in the Second Passage are on the run, pursuing careers, making a living, raising the kids, trying to pay for the house or car or perhaps just the daily food. The very tidal surge that carries them along also washes the gloss off all their dreams.

Grace and Ron Chevington were literally being swept out to sea by this wave. As both of their careers drew them further and further apart, their differences glared openly. The tide had washed off the new gloss to their marriage, leaving behind a tarnished, worn surface. Their challenge was to make this new surface shine again. It would take a lot more than just elbow grease.

Bruce Baldwin in his article "Getting Better—Together" (*USAir Magazine:* August 1990) talks about how this tidal surge can be detrimental to a union in this period:

"Most marriages begin with the highest priority placed on being together and enjoying one another. As the years pass, two destructive priorities slowly take precedence: To make more money so there can be more and more 'things,' and to spend all available time getting chores done. The net result is that a marital relationship slips to the absolute bottom of the priority list.''

In order to work now, the marriage requires time and effort, the two commodities in shortest supply during this busiest season of life. Some couples may unconsciously ask themselves, ''Is my marriage worth precious time and effort?'' It no longer seems to be providing all that the happy couple expected on their wedding day. Quite probably, their career(s) aren't panning out according to their dreams, either. They're growing in directions the couple did not anticipate and perhaps do not want. What about the kids? They aren't as manageable and simple as a parent would like.

Now, too, is the time the partners start taking each other for granted. Add to that complacency the familiarity of sex; no longer is it an exploration. The same old marital partners engage in the same old sexual practices. The gloss, the new, has worn off intimacy as well. Too often, disillusionment replaces the sparkle of young love.

The Anatomy of the First Task

Hercules, son of Zeus and a mortal Greek maiden, Alcmena, was tough enough to rip the shoes off a horse. He strangled two snakes while yet an infant, and you know how hard it is to choke a snake. He killed a huge, ferocious lion and then wore its skin (if you couldn't be barbaric 2700 years ago, when could you?). His next trial was to slaughter the Hydra, the monster possessing nine heads. The middle head was immortal, but that was not the only challenge. Every time Hercules lopped off one head, two sprouted in its place. Try as he might, he could not defeat the beast. Eventually he slew the Hydra by burning the heads off one by one. The immortal head he buried beneath a huge boulder, presumably somewhere around the Mediterranean. That deathless, disembodied head still lies beneath the rocks, mumbling unkind epithets about the mighty man, Hercules.

Sometimes, as reality sinks in and the first blush of true love fades in a marriage, problems seem like the Hydra—but you couldn't feel less like Hercules. Master one little difficulty and two bigger ones pop up. Strive with all your might and the monster looms larger than before. Try as you will, you cannot defeat the beast.

That mythical Hydra is a marriage eater and the "seven year itch" no myth. Statistically, the highest divorce rate hovers somewhere around that seventh-year period. All too often, no one sees it coming. In our practice, we frequently talk to friends and relatives of the divorcees. Over and over, these people, the persons theoretically closest to the divorcing partners, sit in shocked surprise. "What went wrong?" they moan. "Those two seemed so happy."

The Hydra can be bested at this crucial time in a marriage, but it must be slain the way Hercules managed it: Burn off one head at a time.

The major heads of our marriage Hydra are Doubt, Anxiety, Polarization, and Boredom, most of which enter marriage during the Second Passage when reality has set in.

Doubt

Julia Karris giggled self-consciously. "I don't really believe this pop psychology stuff in the magazines, but . . ."

But.

"But this silly little quiz thing confirms doubts I've harbored for a long time. I realize I'm romanticizing my former marriage with Rick; ten years later, it just doesn't seem quite as bad as it seemed at the time. Know what I mean?"

We certainly do know. We hear this stream of thought constantly from different people.

She went on. "Right now with Jerry I'm feeling the same doubts I did with Rick. 'Did I marry the right person?' That question haunts me. Sometimes the answer inside me is yes, and a lot of times it's no. What do I do?"

Sooner or later, and usually during this crucial second stage, almost everyone doubts that their choice of marriage partners was the right one. Moreover, they doubt whether this hectic, stressful married life is for them.

The husband is usually under intense pressure, sapping his energy stores, to succeed in his career and provide for his family. Competition in his workplace is heavy. When the wife is also enmeshed in a career with pressures and competition, both spouses feel these stresses.

The wife is strung-out, exhausted, trying to meet her children's, career's, home's, and husband's needs. Too often, her own needs and her husband's are unmet. Current researchers call this the "second shift" for those women who hold down a job and then come home to the family chores.

The wife gets a massive dose of disillusionment as she views the burgeoning loads of laundry, the dirty dishes, and screaming kids at night. One equation we know to be true is:

Disillusionment = Stress

Every part of her life is stressful, with all sorts of demands pulling on her from all directions. Now, too, the husband is thoroughly preoccupied with his job. In essence it's his mistress, in some cases, his escape from this stressful home situation.

Debi Newman remembers these feelings in their marriage, "Brian was so caught up in his career. Everything revolved around it. When we went out to a restaurant, he would dominate the conversation, glowing as he talked about his practice. It was everything to him and I could see that he loved it. I could also see how I began to resent his job, even feel jealous of it."

Now more than ever, husband and wife begin to doubt if they made the right choice. Could they have had something better in life?

We find this doubt to be the biggest factor in Second Passage difficulties. Moreover this doubt usually follows a predictable progression.

First comes the disillusionment. Julia Karris summed it succinctly: "I want closeness from my marriage. Two people linked together intimately. Not just sex, but sharing intimately in all the other dimensions too. Like . . ." she paused a moment, "like mixing black sand with white sand. The grains are still black and white; they haven't lost their individual color; but they make something new that you can't easily separate— grey sand."

"And you didn't get that in your first marriage," we commented.

"No. Rick took; he didn't give. He wouldn't know what it meant to share. At first, I did get it with Jerry. But now Jerry is so wrapped up in his work that I'm strictly second place. It feels like I'm not a part of his world. We don't share anything significant anymore."

"Is Jerry a part of your working world?"

"No. Not at all. He doesn't think much of my job as a mid-level manager. He doesn't badmouth my job, exactly, but he constantly minimizes it. That just drives me right up the wall."

"And you're discouraged because the kind of marriage you want isn't possible."

Julia sat a moment, frowning. "No." The frown intensified. "I'm discouraged because I can't have that kind of marriage with Rick or Jerry. At the back of my mind, I keep wondering, 'Is there someone out there that I *could* have that kind of marriage with?' "

And Julia has just given voice to the next step in the progression of doubt.

Surely there has to be someone better for me. Our happy-ending culture has deeply instilled in us the concept that every Cinderella is entitled to a Prince Charming and vice versa. When the glass slipper breaks, as it must, our eyes shift elsewhere, seeking.

Julia wagged her head. "There isn't anyone else. I've certainly not found someone new. I'm just so afraid I married the wrong person again, and I want to get out while I'm still young enough to have a decent shot at the gold ring. Know what I mean?"

Again, Julia's attitude is one we see constantly. Most persons who are restless in their marriage want only to get out of it. Remarriage is usually not a consideration. They feel anxious to clean up the mistake they believe they've made and go on. Go where? They don't know. "Out" is the operative word.

Still, they are not out, not yet.

"You know," Julia continued, "now that I look back on it, we weren't really in love. It was a rebound situation. We didn't marry because we loved each other, we married because we thought we needed marriage."

Like Julia, people who feel restless and frustrated in this Second Passage start going back through the files of their mind, digging out the reasons why they should not have married in the first place:

"I was too dumb to know I wasn't in love. I was trying to escape from my parents, but I just didn't know it then."

"He's a nerd. Boring. My friends even told me so. But I blinded myself to it. Now my marriage is so boring I can't stand it. It's been one big tragic, continuous mistake."

And on and on the rationalizations go.

Anxiety

Along with doubt comes anxiety, a truly ugly, hard-to-kill head. Anxiety about job performance and career advancement muddles up all the family relationships. A lot of anxiety also stems from the most profound career of all, parenting.

"I love my kids," Julia wails. "I want to do the best I can for them. Kinsley, too. She's my kid now as much as my own are. Bit by bit, Jerry's dumped virtually all the parenting into my lap. And I can't handle it all. I'm not doing enough, and that means not enough is getting done. It worries me sick, what the kids are missing." She scowled and shifted in her chair. "You know, I'm certain he married me just so he wouldn't have to mess with Kinsley. He didn't marry a wife for him, but a mother for Kinsley. And we only have her half the year!"

Polarization

Julia and Jerry typify a basic characteristic of marriage—polarization. So do Grace and Ron Chevington. As one member becomes more dominant, the other becomes more passive. As one becomes more active, the other becomes ever less active. Soon Julia has become Kinsley's only parent. Soon Grace will be doing everything at home.

"If I don't do it, it won't get done," complains the overworked wife who volunteers at the local senior center, manages all the housework and laundry, and also mows the lawn and keeps the flower beds weeded. And she's right. When she doesn't do all that, it doesn't get done, for her husband has, year by year, slipped into the habit of doing less and less.

"Mom runs the house. She runs Dad, she runs the business, she even tries to run the church. And she's not even a deaconess. She tries to run me, but I finally left home. I don't know why Dad lets her be that way so much."

In part, Dad lets it happen because polarization is such an easy and natural trap to fall into.

The characteristics of a polarized couple are not set in cement. Sometimes the spouses subtly shift roles.

We recently dealt with a case that displayed this polarization. The husband started out as the more dominant partner. He made all the decisions. He stood tall, sort of John Wayne-ish. His wife was ill much of the time, so he also felt protective; he felt a need to give in to her, so to speak, to cater to her needs. As it worked out with time, she became the dominant one. It was a very gradual reversal, but the polarization was there. Now she runs the show and John Wayne has become a shrinking violet.

Debi Newman remembers how polarization affected her marriage, "I didn't really notice Brian's temperament before we got married. If someone had told me that Brian was a domineering person, I would not have believed them. 'He's just a good leader,' I would have protested, 'which is one of the things I like about him.' "

She makes a wry smile, "It didn't take long for his domineering nature to come out in our marriage. One evening, he was in his study. I was writing letters in the kitchen and had some music on. He yelled out, asking me to turn down the music. I did, but it wasn't down far enough. He yelled again, I turned it down further. He yelled again, so I turned it down so low, I couldn't even hear it."

She grimaces as she remembers, "Guess what, that wasn't enough. He yelled again, so I finally turned the radio off. I didn't think about it much until later that night, when it started to bother me. I was mad at him for being domineering, but I was also mad at myself for being so eager to do what he wanted me to do. After all, I lived here too.

"Well, we finally talked about it. And this incident has taught me how to stand up for myself in a positive way. If you let someone walk all over you, they will. And it won't bother them because they're not even aware they're doing it. After being married to Brian for seven years, I have a much stronger personality. I am assertive when I need to be. If Brian didn't have the personality he had, I would not have grown in my assertiveness."

Brian Newman admits, "Debi and I must constantly keep an eye on this seesaw of strengths. Every couple must. We don't want this natural tendency to polarize to get so out of hand that one of us becomes miserable. We found that when a relationship polarizes, neither member is happy, not even the dominant member."

In counsel we learned that a lot of Jerry and Julia's arguments centered around parenting techniques. "Jerry draws a hard line, particularly when it comes to spending," Julia explained. "Me, I like to indulge Kinsley a little every now and then. To Jerry, a 9:00 P.M. bedtime doesn't mean 9:01. I guess I tend to lean towards leniency."

Newlyweds tend to tread lightly with each other, still uncertain of the parameters, still unfamiliar with the intricacies of this many-faceted partner. But by the Second Passage, as the years together bring growth and familiarity, the partners know enough to complement each other, sometimes too well. As one backs off, the other moves forward. When one leaves some slack, as Jerry did with parenthood duties, the other takes it up.

Classically, as this polarization proceeds, the burdened one— Julia in this case—often becomes resentful, and the untrammeled one—Jerry—fails to notice anything has changed.

What About You?

Is your own marriage polarized? Almost automatically, we can say "yes." Everyone polarizes to an extent. Is your marriage *too* polarized? When one spouse is frustrated about the situation, yes. In our example of the mom who ran the whole show, Dad and the whole family felt frustrated and put off. Think about your own marriage. What are the opportunities for work or play that have shifted from one spouse's shoulders onto the other's? It's a question to ask yourself now and then throughout your marriage.

Look carefully at each other. How do you see yourself? As aggressive? As passive? How about your mate? We suggest that you and your spouse consider the following polarities. Rate yourselves on these scales (one for the least, ten for the greatest).

How You See Yourself

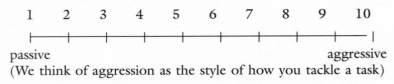

passive   aggressive

(We think of aggression as the style of how you tackle a task)

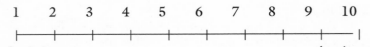

submissive   dominant

(Dominant is different from aggressive, because it involves a desire to take charge of someone else. Do you want your spouse to hear your opinion or does he or she have to agree with you?)

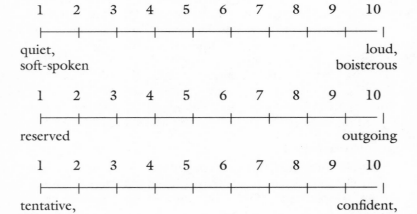

quiet,   loud,
soft-spoken   boisterous

reserved   outgoing

tentative,   confident,
uncertain   bold

How You See Your Spouse

Now rate your spouse on the same characteristics on the scales below:

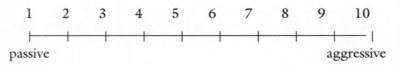

passive   aggressive

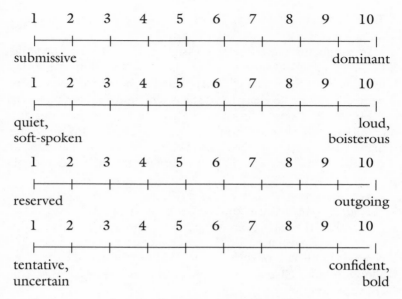

Since many of us tend to marry people who are our opposites, don't be surprised if you rate yourself one way and your spouse the other. People who have different characteristics often complement and compensate for one another.

However, this difference becomes negative when you and your spouse become too polarized. The husband, for instance, can become addictively more and more aggressive, and the wife more and more passive.

We suggest that both spouses rate themselves and each other —and then compare their descriptions as they answer the following three questions.

1. "Do we have a distorted view of each other?"

If each spouse sees the other very differently from the way that person sees himself or herself, then serious distortion is occurring in the relationship. A couple that can't reach consensus as to how they see each other and themselves may need counseling.

2. "How extreme is the polarization between us?"

Obviously, if one spouse sees himself as extremely passive and his wife as extremely dominant, the polarization between them might have become destructive to the relationship.

3. "Even though we are different, do we complement each other or compensate for each other?"

In some marriages both spouses will see the husband as "dominant, loud, aggressive, in charge," and both are comfortable with that. The wife may want to be married to a husband who will take charge and she is willing to be more passive.

However, if one or both of the parties expresses strong discomfort with that relationship, then a change needs to be made. The wife may say, "I believe that you are basically in charge of this marriage. I've put up with it, but I feel buried, overwhelmed."

We often suggest that a couple talk about the areas that need changing. One wife in our counsel asked her husband, "Do you realize that any time we go out, you always become the center of conversation?" Then she negotiated the following change: "One out of three times, I'd like to see you intentionally withdraw. Give me the opportunity to establish myself in conversation."

Boredom

Complacency, the disease of the Second Passage, is, for all practical purposes, a form of boredom. What was once new is commonplace, and there is nothing new and exciting to take its place.

Sex becomes a mechanical thing with a specific purpose. Assume just the right position, do it at exactly the right time. The man begins to feel used. So preoccupied is she, the woman neither feels very sexy nor comes across as such. Boredom results.

Now, think about the sum of these numbers:

- one woman losing her sense of sexuality as she ages
- one man wondering if he's still got it. After all, sexual expression in the marriage has become pretty ho-hum
- two restless people out in the workplace, elbow to elbow with other restless men and women
- lots of stress at home with the kids
- lots of doubts and disillusionments
- a dollop of frustration with work, home, everything

The sum: considerable potential for an affair.

Men and women are sexual creatures, mutually and perhaps unconsciously attracted on that basis alone. Physical proximity encourages that sexual attraction, and men and women are working together more and more in nearly every venue. Should a husband or wife, bored, doubting, and anxious in the marriage relationship find a sympathetic ear of the opposite sex, the attraction multiplies.

"Oh, no!" you proclaim. "My husband and I are Christians. We would never consider something like that."

And we reply, "Sadly, that confers no immunity. Christian, Jew, Buddhist—anyone who holds the marriage vow sacred never considers something like that. Yet in our offices we see so many men and women who ended up in something like that anyway."

The seven-year itch.

What is the best medicine to put on it? What's the cure?

Surviving Realism

Combine our cultural desire for a quick fix with the lack of social pressure to remain married, and you would expect a rise in the divorce rate. It would seem that no class or category of person is immune to marriage dissolution. The odds of staying married these days are correspondingly abysmal. How can you beat them? The following chapters will look at the underlying reasons for doubt, anxiety, polarization, and boredom; but we also offer some solutions below as stopgap measures to try and prevent these "heads of Hydra" from growing too large.

Acceptance of Yourself and Your Spouse

One of the best ways to begin burning off the "head" of doubt is to strive for unconditional acceptance of your mate and yourself. It is also one of the hardest things for mortal human beings to do. A common misconception throughout marriage is: "My mate needs to change to make me happy." Related is the perception that our lives need to change to make me happy. To tackle these misguided notions you must first take responsibility for your own happiness. Learn to like your-

self and feel proud of your accomplishments. There are many
ways to do this. Take time for yourself, get involved in activities
you enjoy, spend time with special friends. Renew your commitment and relationship with God. It's like the popular
"trite" saying: "Get a life!" Encourage your spouse to do the
same.

Couples should be open to changes in each other. They
should accept that one or the other may become disillusioned
with his/her career and want to change, stop, or start another
career. Healthy marriages adapt to what each partner desires.

Encourage Each Other

A friend of ours spoke this way about his marriage, "I feel
my most important role in my marriage is to encourage my
wife. If I can support her as she chases her dreams, then I have
been a good husband." We should all be so sage. This advice
alone will help burn off the "head" of anxiety. We must be
there for our spouses, encouraging them in whatever they're
doing at the time. Our children need the same encouragement.

Positive reinforcement has gotten much press in the business
world as well as in our schools. Positive reinforcement is even
more critical in our families. Much of our book is devoted to
weeding out and getting rid of the negative pressures on your
relationship. One of the best ways to do that is to shift your
emphasis from focusing on what's wrong with your mate, your
kids, or your relationship, and emphasize what's right. Tell
your wife or husband she/he is doing a good job at parenting
and you're proud of him/her. The same principle applies for
whatever career they're pursuing.

Variety, the Spice of Life

Chores and responsibilities are, unfortunately, a reality that
won't go away. How those mundane items are accomplished,
though, can be varied. One of the ways to avoid polarization is
to change those responsibilities frequently between partners,
especially family chores.

Avoid falling into the rut of always doing the same jobs. Let
the husband cook dinner a few times, even if he has never done
so previously. You might discover the next Grand Chef, or you
might have to choke it down. No matter. Think of the humor

this will invoke—the funny reactions, the antacid. Let the wife mow the lawn and take out the garbage, while the husband gives the kids a bath and does the laundry. Divide up these jobs and vary who does them each week.

Paying bills is no picnic. It somehow seems that no matter how much money a family makes, the same amount of free cash is available—very little. Watching your precious hard-earned salaries trickle out check-by-check to this and that can be downright depressing. Vary who pays the bills each month as well as who balances the checkbook. Both of you will get a real handle on where your money is going and two heads are better than one when budgeting.

If work schedules allow, the husband or wife can do the carpooling of the kids to their activities and become involved in parent-teacher meetings. Share the responsibility of parenting. Both spouses should reap the rewards that this wonderful career, parenting, provides.

Varying these responsibilities and chores will also help burn off the "head" of boredom.

Recommit to Romance

An anomaly in this Second Passage is: the couple now spends more time together than ever before, but not as lovers. Because of the busy schedules they both must keep, they are exhausted. Rarely do they go out now. They spend most of their time at home, doing chores, being with the kids, and watching television.

Avoid spending precious time doing chores. Chores can wait. Turn off the television whenever possible; tape the program on the VCR if need be.

Spend quality time together, take leisurely walks holding hands. Engage in intimate talks together *not* about the kids, the house, the bills, or jobs.

Some couples we know even schedule specific dates each week. In particularly hectic times this may be the only answer. Don't break these dates for anything short of an emergency. Now more than ever, your marriage should be your highest priority, falling only behind your relationship to God and your relationship to yourself. It should even take precedence over the kids. The kids will be happy if your marriage is happy, and you will be giving them an enormous education for their future.

Be creative. Send the kids to a neighbor and surprise your spouse with a romantic, candlelit dinner for two at home. Trade weekend babysitting with friends and get away, just the two of you as honeymooners. Brian and Debi Newman make sure they do this at least once a year. More often would be even better.

Another idea, play games together as a couple. A couple we know play three games of backgammon after dinner. It doesn't happen every single night, because other things intrude; sometimes they're not together, or they have company. The person who's behind at the end of each month buys dinner out for the other.

Plan little surprises for each other. Get the kids involved. Have them help pick out Mom's birthday gift. Special, spontaneous gifts go a long way to promote romance. Funny, quirky gifts, such as tacky men's underwear, can help a bit; even if they won't ever be worn. The man who invented them is now a millionaire.

Commit annually to enriching your marriage. Several of our friends plan and execute marital recommitment ceremonies on major anniversaries, usually reflecting the original wedding ceremony. Seek out and nurture the little secrets you share, private signals that have meaning even in a crowd.

Injecting Humor in Your Family

As the avocado is to guacamole, so is laughter to your family. Many laugh-provoking incidents will involve the children in some way, but equally important are those funny incidents which involve just the two of you.

When you laugh, you feel good, literally, not just psychologically but physiologically as well. Laughter promotes your body's manufacture of endorphins. Endorphins work to relieve pain and spread pleasure throughout your body. Thus, laughter works like a natural tranquilizer and stress reliever.

Charles Swindoll, the beloved author, offers some guidelines for injecting fun in your family. He recommends you keep fun authentic. Manufactured fun is a contradiction in terms. Keep rules and policies as minimal as possible. "Strait-laced" and "rule-rigid" are also counterproductive to flexible creativity. Few women today know the painful, intimate, primary meaning of strait-laced, for corsets, blessedly, have passed from fashion. Suffice to say, tight strictures are not fun. One family we know encourages food fights at dinner. We don't want to imply that everyone should do this, but you get the idea.

Swindoll further suggests that unless it is impossible to say "yes," say "yes," whatever the suggestion. Who knows what delights a wild idea might uncover? And a failure is not the end of the world. If something flops, go to something else. To quote the hackneyed phrase, "If life hands you a lemon, make lemonade."

"Okay," says Grace Chevington, "so exactly where and how do I inject humor and laughter in my marriage? Ron is such a deadbeat! It's a no-win situation. Where do I even start?"

Grace would learn that she and Ron had to work through some very serious issues which we will discuss in our subsequent chapters. But she could begin to inject humor and light-heartedness in their lives now. How?

The dinner table is an excellent place to begin. Lou Ajanian never let TV get in the way of dinner. He and Marj sat at the table and conversed during dinner. Always. (If some family member simply cannot be weaned away from the evening news, use a VCR and time shift; let him or her watch the news after dinner. It won't get that stale in half an hour.) The dinner table is a good laughing place; you know, one of those warm and comfortable places where the family knows it can feel bright and goofy.

Look for small things to celebrate: getting the dog's teeth cleaned; changing the ribbon in your typewriter; the victory of Dad, who's been trying to improve his language at home and work, making it clear through the day without a single profane word; finishing the drywall in the basement; completing a Passage of marriage. There's a lot of things to celebrate. We don't celebrate enough in our world. When something goes right, make a big deal of it. We certainly do it when something goes wrong.

And, for tradition's sake, keep some sort of record of it.

Building Memories

Gloria Gaither and Shirley Dobson's book *Let's Make a Memory* (Dallas: Word, 1983) provides some ideas for building a history of union and laughter in your family. Something out of a book probably won't work unless you approach the whole idea thoughtfully—looking not for cookbook steps but new ideas, then tailoring those ideas to your own unique needs.

Incidentally, if you embark on anything new like this you'll have to learn to disregard complainers. They don't mean it personally. It's just that . . . well . . . so phooey on the complainers. They'll get with the program. And look what they're missing if they opt out of the celebration.

Begin a family history. Start now, it's never too late. Write a letter to each other on every anniversary. Take videos or photographs of special events and also everyday happenings. In every historical collection, the most valuable and telling photos are not of the nabobs standing around shaking hands but of ordinary people in ordinary situations. That's exactly what's given rise to the immensely popular TV show "America's Funniest Home Videos." Your family can provide such funny, entertaining events. Remember your humorous times as a couple during courtship and the early years of marriage, before kids. Tell them to your children, they love to hear about Mom and Dad—what they did, how they got in or out of trouble, how they are human too and make mistakes.

Take a vacation. A few years ago, Frank Minirth was startled by his daughter's lament, "We never take a vacation." Actually, the family went many places in the course of a year, but the excursions were always work related. Frank had a conference here or a speaking engagement there, and would take the family along. His daughter, though, wanted a real vacation. "You know, Dad, where nobody has to do anything." He makes certain the family gets a vacation once a year now, a real vacation where nobody has to do anything.

Most importantly, examine your family traditions. We are a tradition-bound people, all of us, and our traditions in large measure define us. From a recent *National Geographic* (February, 1991) article on a people of southwestern Ethiopia, under government pressure to modernize, comes this quote from the

Surma: "We don't want to give up body painting, stick fighting, or lip plates. This is our way of life. We want to keep it and pass it on to our children."

Hold fast to those traditions and pass them on to your children. A friend of ours, of Scandinavian ancestry, once described the Christmas Eve tradition at her house.

"Everyone eats lutefisk . . ." she began.

"Lutefisk. Isn't that a fish dish of some sort?"

"We keep telling Dad, 'Hey, our ancestors didn't eat this stuff because it's festive. They ate it because it was the only thing they had in the middle of winter. This is starvation rations, Pop.' "

"But Pop pulls rank?"

"To the max. 'It's tradition,' he says. So we eat the stuff. Then Pop puts on his helmet . . ."

"With horns?"

"Cow horns, yeah. Classic Viking. And we sing the old songs. It's hokey and camp, and we've always loved it."

We've always loved it. Grown and gone from home, she and her brothers and sisters are passing the tradition, including the lutefisk, on to their children. It's an annual event steeped in a long history of humor and fame among their friends and relatives.

As easy as these stopgap measures sound, none of them will be effective if you haven't also examined the underlying reasons for strife in your marriage. In the following chapters we will explore these reasons and provide ways for you to undo or prevent their happiness-damaging effects. One of the most obvious changes in a marriage occurs when the kids arrive.

Chapter 4

And Now
the Kids

"**A**rnold," he grimaced. "They went and named me Arnold. You know the only way you can go through school as an Arnold is if your last name is Schwarzenegger. Even my name works against me."

In our office, frail, slim, balding Arnold sat in his chair in a knot. Not only were his legs crossed, but the toe of one foot wound around behind the other leg—a double cross. His crossed arms tightly guarded his heart. Arnold was not a happy man.

"Tell us about your first wife," we asked.

"What's to tell? We were married nine years. Then things turned against me. I was a pastor. I guess she got tired of playing second fiddle to the entire congregation. She left."

"Children?"

"Three. She has custody. Except holidays."

"Let's talk about your chil—"

"And my birthday."

"Beg your pardon?"

"My birthday. The kids get to visit on my birthday. Also on Washington's and Lincoln's birthdays." He shifted in his chair and retied his body knots.

We nodded. "How old are your—"

"And Columbus Day. Some schools get out on the Monday

when the banks close, and some celebrate the actual day, October 12. No uniformity. So I got it in writing that the kids visit on the legal holiday, whenever that falls. I work in a bank, you see—I had to resign my pastorate during the divorce—and I wanted the guarantee that I have the day off when the kids are here."

"What do you do in the bank?"

"Advise churches and other nonprofit organizations about investments. I'm considered very good at it. Our bank has seen a 27 percent increase in investment accounts in the last year, and nearly all are with nonprofit institutions. Special rules, you know. It's not your usual investment strategy."

"Your experience as a pastor must be invaluable in that line of work."

"Exactly!" And Arnold launched into a detailed explanation of IRS rulings and the difference between various investments such as Fanny Maes and Ginny Maes. We drew him back to the subject of his children, learning eventually that they were aged eight, six, and four.

He seemed to loosen a little, and his face sagged, sadder. "There was a lot of financial pressure when I was pastoring, and time pressures, and other demands. Kids take so much time, and add to that—confusion. The house was always in an uproar, and a pastor lives in a fishbowl. You know that. Appearances are so important. What will the neighbors think? Kids give nosy neighbors a lot to think about."

He grimaced again. "Ironic. It's all against me. Each year the kids get older, they cost more. More money. More time. Now that I'm making a better-than-decent living at an eight-hour-a-day job, I don't have the kids anymore."

Kids—and the lack of kids if they've always been a part of your dreams for your family—raise the stress level of any marriage. The second task in the Second Passage of marriage is to childproof your marriage.

Task Two: Childproof Your Marriage

"It's a dangerous myth," says Debi Newman, "that having a baby will help save a marriage. Babies add enormous stress."

A formula we will expound on later is:

$$1 \text{ person} + 1 \text{ person} = \text{conflict}$$
$$\text{and}$$
$$1 \text{ person} + 1 \text{ person} + 1 \text{ more person} = \text{more conflict}$$

You can see that adding one member promises friction by multiplying the possible combinations. Mom mothers, but at times she also fathers. Dad fathers, but occasionally must assume the mother role. And then there is each adult's private life individually—work, the world outside the home—and their life as a sexually united couple.

Tossing one child into the pot multiplies the opportunities for friction exponentially, and most families have more than one child, all interacting in a multitude of roles. There's more opportunity to disagree, more power struggles, more differences of taste and preferences, both within and between the generations. Children have many more needs than do adults; needs to be emotionally nurtured on the road to adulthood (and that's not just a pat on the head in passing). Kids have intense needs that must be met immediately.

Kids introduce another negative element too: from the parents' viewpoint, they provide more opportunity to fail. The woman with low self-esteem, the man who is unsure of himself, not only faces the possibility of being considered a bad spouse, but a bad parent as well. And those two occupations are pursuits the world thinks ought to come naturally.

Brian and Debi Newman comment, "Over and over in counseling we see parents react out of a fear of failure. But they don't actually acknowledge that fear of failure. Thus they don't realize the grip it has on them."

"We've all felt the pull to give in to our children's temper tantrums in the store, just to keep people from staring and wondering what kind of parents we are," says Debi Newman. "A more extreme example is the mother who was overweight as a teenager. She may now fear that her child will become overweight and experience the same rejection she experienced in childhood. When she sees her three-year-old daughter enjoying food and eating healthily, the mother may panic and try to take away the food, not realizing the power plays or feelings she may be creating in her daughter."

Still More Pressure

This multiplicity of personalities, with all the frictions and quirks, is the least of the stress. As Arnold realized, children apply financial pressures from conception on. No parent needs to be told the bewildering variety of ways kids cost money, and non-parents don't want to know.

Children do not sit quietly in a corner. They get involved in activities—sports, clubs, myriad activities to crunch the already-busy parents' time and energy.

In the course of these activities, children meet other adults. As a necessary part of growing up, the kids forge strong personal relationships with some of them. When these relationships reach worshipful proportions, (and there is a brief, normal period in every child's life when just such a relationship happens) the parents often feel jealous or threatened. Because this bond sneaks in, unexpected, unprepared-for, the jealousy causes even more friction and damage.

The Shifting Sands of Parenthood

As rapidly as a newborn child changes, the parents change also. And the maturation is as predictable and certain in the parent as it is in the child. The maturation can be broken down into five stages, which obviously do not parallel the marriage passages we've discussed in Chapter 1. We will discuss two of these stages—the period of surprise (the first child) and the period of drifting (school-age children) in this Second Passage of marriage. The other three stages—the stage of turmoil (adolescent children), the stage of renewal or death of relationship (the empty nest), and the stage of joy (grandchildren) will be covered in our other books on later passages of marriage.

The Period of Surprise—The First Child

The surprise factor, summarized, is the way that third little person multiplies the happiness and the stress of the family's interrelationships.

Julia Karris gave voice to one element of surprise. "I baby-sat when I was kid. But then you go home. Even with brothers and sisters, you never realize how a baby ties you down. Every moment the baby's either with you, or you've arranged for him or her to be with someone. There's no off-time, no time to walk away from a baby."

Carl Warden wagged his head over the memories of another element of surprise. "I remember our first one. Annie was actually an easy kid as babies go. Still, parenthood was nothing like what I expected. I don't know what I expected, but this sure wasn't it. And I didn't get the worst of it. Annie was two years old when I got home from overseas. Bess took the brunt of it.

"I mean, here's this tiny person all over the house, babbling, insisting you listen to her, play with her, read to her, tugging on your pants leg, fussing.

"But the biggest surprise was the power struggles. A child three feet high can't read or write or mow the lawn, yet you get into this powerful contest of wills. Bess and I would get into power struggles, too, over Annie. I don't know how parents ever get past the first child."

Power struggles—that old question, "Who's in control here?" now rephrased to "Who's in control of this child?"—can indeed unravel the marriage fabric. Power struggles also offer, however, the potential to improve intimacy. Struggles are, in effect, a form of conflict and can be dealt with as the parents would deal with other conflicts. Negotiation between the parents reveal the parents' thoughts and preferences to each other. As the problem is ironed out, each gets to know the other a little better.

One solid principle for keeping kids from damaging the marital bond is for spouses to agree upon their philosophy of child-raising before the fact, not after the kids come along and generate a crisis. The parents should agree in advance on a united front. If that sounds like a war strategy, it is. Kids will divide you if they can, to gain their own ends.

How About You?

In counseling we suggest that couples review the parenting they observed in their family of origin. Take a moment to think about how your parents' actions affect your attitudes toward raising children by checking the statements below that apply to you:

_____ "In my family children were encouraged to voice their opinions concerning family decisions."

_____ "In my family children were given an allowance tied to their chores."

_____ "In my family everyone ate something different at mealtimes."

_____ "In my family sons were treated differently from daughters."

_____ "In my family both my mom and dad would try to attend my sports, school, and church functions."

_____ "My father (or mother) didn't pay much attention to me."

_____ "In my family the father was the person who disciplined the children."

_____ "In my family it was okay to spank the children."

_____ "My parents would get angry and slap the children."

Now take a look at your own beliefs about child raising:

_____ "I believe children need to learn how to manage money as they grow up."

_____ "I believe that it is all right for children to talk back to their parents."

_____ "I believe that both father and mother should be involved in the daily care of the children."

_____ "I believe that it is important for children to be involved in extra activities, like dancing, sports, and piano lessons."

_____ "How children behave and their manners are very important to me."

_____ "I believe that both parents should discipline the kids."

_____ "I plan to spank our children as a way of discipline."

_____ "I want our family to hold and hug each other."

Compare your responses to these statements with the first set you checked on your family of origin. Which of your attitudes about child rearing has been influenced by your parents? Is that influence good or bad? Now discuss these issues with your spouse. Once you have talked through your thoughts about child rearing and how they have been influenced, for better or for worse, by your parents, we suggest that the two of you enter into a verbal or written covenant concerning child rearing. Consider a verbal or written agreement like the one below:

- "I agree that we should use consistent child-rearing techniques and discipline in all cases."
- "I promise to discuss any child-rearing issues with you privately and never in front of our children."
- "I promise never to contradict your discipline of our children in front of them. If I am confused about a method you have used, I will discuss it privately with you and clarify it with our children after our discussion."
- "I believe that both of us should be involved in the daily care of the children."
- "I agree to discuss with you how much extra activities our children will be involved in."
- "I agree that we should share the discipline of our children equally."
- "I agree that how children behave and their manners at home and away from home are very important to both of us."

You may want to add to or change these statements as you and your spouse wish. Remember, however: With young children, the goal is not democracy. The children are not part of this covenant. It is critical that the parents be parents and let the children be children. In counseling we find two situations that usually begin right in this first period of parenthood, and either situation can irreversibly damage both the marriage and the children.

Fear of Rejection

We are constantly amazed and dismayed at how deeply some parents fear their kids will cease to like them. One of our clients, Amy Marchand, tells her story:

"I suppose every mother worries that maybe her kid will turn out hating her. Look at how children scream and holler when you want them to do something they don't want to. Or tell them no.

"When my little Pete yelled 'Mommy, I hate you!' one day, I think that's what really got me. Pete wanted to play in the mud around the storage shed we were building out back. It was nap time and I didn't want him to get dirty. He threw a fit when I tried to drag him inside, and then he said that.

"I'm ashamed to admit it now, but then I guess I was just shocked. I turned him loose and he ran back to the mud hole. It wasn't long before all he had to do was screech once and we'd give in, my husband and I both. The more we let him have his way, the more we tried to please him, the worse he got."

We asked Amy this question: "If you were to crack down and enforce reasonable discipline, do you think he'd hate you?"

She replied, "Yes. He's too used to having his own way."

"Does he really love you now?"

"No."

"Then what will you lose?"

Another situation that can cause disaster in a family is the parenting technique where the kids are given more responsibility than they should have at their level of maturity.

Emotional Incest

When children come into a marriage from prior marriages, the conflict shoots up even higher. Joel and Carolyn found that out the hard way.

Carolyn sat in our office on the verge of tears. "Joel is wonderful. I realize every bride who's only been married eight months is going to say that, but he really is. He's so—so mellow. My former husband, Ralph, was verbally abusive. Extremely so. Our daughter Michelle grew up in a constant state of terror."

Even though Carolyn had only been married eight months, she was already in the Second Passage of marriage since this was a second marriage and she and her husband had children from a previous marriage. Her problems were not as unique as she thought.

"How old is Michelle now?" we asked.

"Almost fourteen. I met Joel at Michelle's sixth-grade open house. His Janna was in the same class. Michelle seemed thrilled that Janna's dad and me were getting together. Michelle was our biggest booster."

"But when you married, her attitude changed."

"Did it ever. There's a lot of jealousy. Joel's kids are jealous because they can't live with him, and they make life miserable every time we have them. Okay, I can see that. But Michelle's got it made. Her natural father yelled at her and put her down all the time. Joel doesn't do any of that. She *wanted* us to make a family. And now . . ."

It's a pattern we see so often. "How is she acting out?"

"Big mouth, talking back. Boys. It's the boys that worry me most."

"Other than Michelle, everything's going all right?"

Carolyn brightened. "Before I ever met Joel I had already worked through most of the issues associated with the first marriage. Counseling, Michelle and I both went. We pretty much got our heads on straight, finally. Joel and I appreciate each other more than most couples do because we've both been around the block. We really have a good thing going, with a lot of work."

So what could go wrong? We talked to Carolyn's daughter, Michelle. In the years of living alone with her mother, Michelle had learned to depend upon Mom. She thereby felt safe as never before. Mom supported her. Mom wouldn't let her down. Unfortunately, Mom developed almost exactly the same dependency upon her daughter. Mom needed Michelle for affirmation. She needed Michelle to pick up the slack when life and work got too much. Michelle became the confidante, a job she was too young and ill-equipped to handle. When the child nurtures the parent, as Michelle nurtured her mom, we call it emotional incest.

We are seeing that emotional incest, the transfer of intimacy from spouse to child, is the single most damaging thing that kids bring to a marriage; and it's not their fault. Kids must be allowed to be kids, without the responsibility and onus of assuming quasi-parental or quasi-spousal roles.

Emotional incest seems particularly prevalent among divorced families. Parents with primary custody are under severe pressure. They are handling the jobs of two parents at once, and they are also dealing with all the issues the divorce invoked in themselves and their children. When they meet a new person and remarry, the children really heat up the situation.

Stepparenting

Julia Karris's children from her first marriage, Angela and Greg, lived with her and Jerry for part of the year. So did Kinsley Karris, Jerry's daughter from his first marriage. Their times didn't always overlap. It sounds like a logistical nightmare. It is. And it's too often a reality for many second marriages.

Early in Jerry and Julia's marriage, Greg caused problems. At twelve he was just beginning his "hormonal" chaos and he intensely resented his stepfather. His mom had cared for him and his sister during most of his grade school years. She had even referred to Greg as the "man of the house" now. Greg liked that. But when Jerry entered the picture that all changed. Now there was a new "man of the house." Even though Greg might have been relieved he no longer had to have all that responsibility, he was extremely jealous of his mom's "new" man.

Add to this boiling stew the original father and Greg's and Angela's feelings for him. After all they spent some of the year with him. Suddenly a new person was thrust upon them. How were they supposed to feel about him? He sure wasn't their father.

We could devote an entire book to this subject alone. We won't even attempt an in-depth treatment here. You may want to read *The Father Book* by Dr. Frank Minirth, Dr. Brian Newman, and Dr. Paul Warren (Nashville: Thomas Nelson, 1992) for a more comprehensive discussion of this subject.

However, for this book's purposes, let us briefly discuss the progression of stepparent relationships. Dr. Newman categorizes this progression into six distinct phases.

One theme remains constant throughout: The focus should be on the marriage! What will ultimately benefit the children, be they yours biologically or not, is a strong marriage between you and your spouse.

Phase 1—Fantasy Phase

This occurs during the First Passage of marriage, when new love is in full bloom. The kids have been desperate for a mother or father, a complete family. To them, a two-parent family is a fantasy they have been dreaming of ever since the divorce. Finally, here it is!

Phase 2—Competitive Phase

Children, and the parents for that matter, rarely foresee problems and frictions. Paintings of the mind are exceedingly rosy. Reality is not. As the reality sinks in, the kids start to resent the new family member. Is the child being disloyal to the birth parents if he or she loves this stepparent? The child's dilemma is complicated as parents and stepparents embroil in competition with each other for the children's love. To their dismay, the kids realize that their fantasy about this new two-parent family does not reflect reality. They often perceive a true situation much faster than do adults.

"If I like Jerry, will my dad think I don't love him anymore?" Greg thought. Add to that his dad's comments about his ex-wife's new husband. They weren't very complimentary, and Greg and Angela heard them over and over every time they visited their dad.

Small wonder that in this phase kids start exhibiting behavioral problems. "I just can't handle Greg anymore," Julia complained. "He's out all hours, never home. When he is home, he snaps at me and ignores Jerry."

Jerry Karris was overwhelmed. How could he discipline Greg, who wasn't even his kid? Whenever he tried, Greg lashed back with, "My *real* father would never do this." Soon Jerry began to doubt his own capability as a parent. He shifted more and more of the parenting responsibilities to Julia, including responsibility for his own daughter Kinsley.

Incidentally, the response to "You're not my mom (or dad)!" is simply, "Nope. You're right. But I am in charge here." All stepparents must recognize that they will never fully take the place of the biological father or mother, let alone be the father or mother. For the kids' sake, they must never attempt to usurp that position.

As the strains mount, the marriage enters the Second Passage and reality sinks in big time. This phase of stepparenting slips into the next phase.

Phase 3—Instant Family

Head knowledge versus heart knowledge. The heads of all these stepfamily members always knew they were blending an instant family. Of course, obvious, but it never quite sunk in to heart level. As the Second Passage rolls onward, the new spouse suddenly realizes at heart-depth that he or she has acquired an instant family with all its existing problems and hidden issues. The new spouse feels like an outsider more and more. Kids exacerbate the outsider feeling with covert messages saying "You're not really welcome here. Things were just fine until you showed up." The children may even look to their biological mother or father to protect them from this interloper.

Julia Karris, guilt-ridden about forcing Jerry into her children's lives, allowed Greg to run rampant, until it got out of hand. Anything Jerry did to try and stop that was ignored by Greg and unsupported by Julia. Greg, the kid with a mom and two dads, ended up without functional parents.

At this phase, the kids may try to sabotage the new relationship in a desperate attempt to get their mom and dad back together again. Rarely is this sabotage a conscious effort. For example, every time Jerry Karris tried to warm up to ten-year-old Angela, she rejected him. Angela couldn't accept Jerry as a parent. In her mind, if she did, it meant that Mommy and Daddy wouldn't get back together again.

By this stage, the mythical Hydra of Chapter 3 seems indestructible. Every time the new parent makes a small step forward, four more things go wrong. An uneasy situation turns into a catastrophe.

This is why we recommend, in the strongest terms, that stepfamilies seek outside help at this phase or before—professional counseling, a pastor, a good friend, anyone who can provide an objective viewpoint. The spouses are simply too close to the problems to identify what's wrong.

Phase 4—Explosion and Conflict

If a stepfamily has not sought outside guidance, the fourth phase can erupt violently. The marriage may well fall as a casualty to the explosion. By now, the stepparent feels in direct competition with the kids, not only for their affection, but for the spouse's attention. The kids usually position themselves between their mom or dad and their stepdad or stepmom. It's all-out war.

The kids also receive mixed messages. They may be migrating between two households with two very different rules and regulations. Consistency is out the window and consistency is crucial for kids.

Phase 5—Make It or Break It

This phase is the climax, the turning point of stepfamilies. Either the marriage is going to make it or it will fall apart. The couple will either seek counseling or outside support or they will separate.

Julia and Jerry Karris fortunately sought help. We focused on their marriage first and foremost. Our goal was to solidify this union. We had to make this their goal as well if we were to succeed.

"We're in this together," Julia and Jerry eventually agreed. "We want to work this out."

Good. We could begin.

Jerry and Julia Karris had to go through all the Second Passage issues and tasks and also deal with the stepparenting issues. It would be a difficult but rewarding experience for both of them. This step led them to the final phase of stepparenting. . .

Phase 6—Resolution

Here is the light at the end of the tunnel. The stepfamily fortunate enough to reach this phase enjoys a strong chance of survival. By now, the roles of each family member are clarified and brought out in the open. Stepdad relaxes the intense, unrealistic expectations he had as father and husband and head of the household. He no longer need be all those roles perfectly. Stepmom comes to realize she can't juggle everything and make it all come out neatly. She learns to accept the warts and scars of a less-than-perfect union and go with what she has. Neither is Superparent anymore.

The kids settle in to the sad realization that life isn't going to be perfect for them, either. Their dreams of the original family are dead. This new family is the reality. They must work out the kinks of loving two sets of parents and of being loved, or ignored, as the case may be. The key: We're in this *together*.

A very necessary part of Task Two (Childproofing Your Marriage) if you are in a step situation is to work through these six phases. But what happens if your marriage is devoid of children? Kids can also raise the chaos level in a marriage when the couple seems unable to have children.

Pressure When the Nest Stays Empty

Many women have trouble conceiving and carrying a child to term. Some suffer miscarriage for physiological reasons. This inability to have children puts another kind of stress on the marriage.

Mary Alice Minirth knows that stress well. "Our first pregnancy and miscarriage, I didn't know it happened. Frank was in his third year of medical school," she recalls. "I was teaching in an inner-city ghetto. I thought my period was messed up from the stress, but I actually miscarried a pregnancy. Not long after that Frank was diagnosed with diabetes, and his future became uncertain. My father had cancer. It was the lowest I've ever been.

"We tried again. I suffered three miscarriages in two and a half years. I was trying to teach in that stressful situation, and I felt hopeless. Everyone else was having kids. After a miscarriage, I'd get on the elevator to go home and see a mother with a baby in her arms. I'd get in the car and just cry.

"Some doctors and friends advised us to hang it up. Quit trying. They'd say 'Aw, move on. It's over.' But it's a severe loss."

Frank agrees. "Miscarriage is much more of an issue than most people will admit. It's a severe loss, and you have to go through the stages of grief. A husband must be supportive of his wife. He has to try to understand her emotions because he probably has them also. Her emotions add insight into his own feelings. He may not realize how much the loss is affecting him. It is. Men tend to lack a keen awareness of their own emotions. It's not that they're not emotional; it's just that, in general, men are not as acutely aware of their feelings as women are. Also, talk about the loss. Listening and being listened to are the strongest medicines available."

Grieving the Loss

A friend of ours miscarried because she didn't understand how certain chemicals could affect the unborn child's health. "I was two months pregnant when it happened," she said. "Dumb old us, we didn't know that some kinds of paint fumes can induce spontaneous abortion. We were refinishing some furniture, and I got sick from it and miscarried." She stared at her hands in her lap. "I always wonder what the baby would have been like."

"When did this happen?" we asked.

Her eyes brimmed with tears. "Twenty-five years ago."

The loss of an unborn child requires a special kind of grieving because of the unknown. What would that child have been like? Who would the little one have become? To the husband even more so than the wife, that little one is nothing more than a theory, a loss described without ever being seen or touched. Parents of unborn children add other factors in as they work through their grief.

The first step of the grief process, is *shock and denial*. Mary Alice received a particularly hard jolt when she learned that her "abnormal period" and its consequence was the loss of her first pregnancy. The jolt can be even more severe for a couple who learns of the pregnancy, anticipates the new arrival, and then watches the dream shatter, as the Minirths did during the next three pregnancies.

Feelings run deep and painful. Anger is entirely appropriate. Never let someone try to talk you out of an emotional response with, "It's only a tadpole at that stage," or "It's not the end of the world" (for at this moment, it is), or the cruelest of all, "You (will) have other children. It's not so bad." It is so bad! A death is a death.

The second step is *depression*. Mary Alice Minirth recalls, "I felt hopeless about my past, present, and future. I was almost clinically depressed. I wanted to sleep a lot." This step may be complicated by physiological factors. A woman's hormones alter during pregnancy, and with them her emotional state and balance. Should you lose a child, your body's hormones are thrown for a loop. The physical condition can cause depression apart from the depression of the grieving process. If depression becomes exceedingly severe or lingers far too long (months and months), seek medical help. But do expect depression. It's normal.

The third step, *bargaining*, must not be confused with the advice to never give up hope, and certainly not with prayer. "Lord, please give me a child" is not the same as "Lord, if you just give me a child, I'll _____ in return." Bargaining and magical thinking are part of grieving and should be temporary in nature. Guard, though, against letting one of your bargains or magical thoughts turn into a plan of action. Magic won't help you.

Sadness. Losing an unborn child is so sad. Again, you may receive all sorts of sincere but very wrong advice, particularly if your sadness shows clearly or persists a while. Besides, you're overcoming the medical effects of the loss, just as would a woman who gave birth. That makes it all the harder. It is natural and necessary to feel great sadness; let no one tell you otherwise.

The final phases of grieving, *forgiveness and resolution,* bring a measure of peace, but they do not close the book or erase memories. Whom should you forgive? In the case of the woman who inhaled paint fumes, she had to forgive her and her husband's ignorance which led to the miscarriage. It was not a deliberate act, but it required forgiveness *for the woman's sake.* If a person was instrumental in causing the miscarriage, such as a reckless driver responsible for an accident in which the unborn baby died, that person must be forgiven—again, *for the couple's sake.* Not forgotten. Not let off the hook. But forgiven.

Forgiveness is so vital in a healthy relationship that we will discuss the anatomy and how-to's of this misunderstood concept in detail later.

Resolution is the healthy outcome of the grieving process.

How did Mary Alice resolve her grief? "Two things," she explains. "Keep going, and never abandon hope.

"I'm thinking now of Mrs. Winger, a godly lady. She and her surgeon husband came over to me and said, 'I really know God's got good things for you.' God used Frank to encourage me too. He kept me moving forward, putting one foot in front of the other. In spite of what friends and doctors said, we kept hoping. I had one Christian doctor who said 'never give up.'

But then there was also a pastor's wife who told me, 'Maybe it's your genes.' This was right in the middle of the church building! So you pick up the positive advice and feedback, and don't listen to the negative things."

Frank echoes the maxim, "Don't believe the message of no hope! God can provide. But you have to open the door to Him."

Trying involves developing a plan of action. "Frank knew how sad and depressed I was," Mary Alice says, "so one day he sat me down and said that, with God's help, we would have a child. 'We will do everything we can—including going to an adoption agency—and then we will leave the rest up to God.' "

Six months later, when Mary Alice became pregnant again, they regrouped. "Frank's plan was for me to stay on the sofa all nine months if I had to. I organized drawers to keep busy. I read the whole Living Bible. It's the last time I did any embroidery."

At three months the Minirths were able to hear the baby's heartbeat. The next two months—the times when Mary Alice had miscarried before—went by without incident. At five months Mary Alice was able to buy maternity clothes for the first time. Everything went well until the thirty-second week of pregnancy when the doctor said that Mary Alice was showing signs of premature labor.

Mary Alice Minirth spent the last six weeks of that fourth pregnancy in the hospital. "It was a frightening time because I imagined that every little pain would lead to stronger labor pains and to a premature baby. And, all along, I feared that the baby would not be healthy. After six weeks, the labor pains seemed to stop." Yet eight and a half months had finally gone by and the baby could arrive any time.

Two weeks later Rachel Marie Minirth was born, a healthy, seven-pound, eleven-ounce, bright-eyed baby. Frank and Mary Alice Minirth had been married seven years. They named their little girl Rachel because of the verse in Genesis that says, "So Jacob served seven years for Rachel, and they seemed but a few days to him because of the love he had for her" (Gen. 29:20). Both Frank and Mary Alice felt that God had worked out His plan for their lives in His own way and His own timing.

"We lost one other baby after Rachel," Mary Alice says. "It

was right after we moved to Dallas. It was excruciating, too, because it went on for three weeks. Lose it or save it? We lost it. But God had given us Rachel, so there was hope. Frank had his career, a new life to look forward to, a new practice. We had a new home and we had company all summer, too, which kept me busy. Old friends. It kept me going after the miscarriage.

"I think I had to fight self-pity most. We had so much, yet I didn't see it. You're blinded to what you have when you're in despair over what you don't have. I kept showing myself I had friends, and one child coming into her two's, and we had a worthy goal in life. God was opening up things for Frank.

"By the time our second child was born healthy, my father's cancer was arrested. He lived a full and happy life for many more years."

Today the Minirths have four girls: Rachel, age 17; Renee, age 14; Carrie, age 11; and Alicia, age 2. During this latest pregnancy, as with the others, Mary Alice spent months resting on the couch and Frank suspended any travel outside of Dallas so he could support her and help with the older girls.

Together the Minirths grieved the loss of four unborn babies and together they share the joy of their four lovely daughters. They have experienced the challenges of raising children through various stages, including "the period of drifting."

The Period of Drifting—School-Age Kids

We call this a period of drifting for several reasons. For one, it seems the family members are each cast adrift, going separate ways, aimlessly. For all the churning activity, you see very little real progress day to day. In fact, with school-age kids, how do you measure progress, if any?

Also, the family itself tends to drift. Pressed severely by all the issues school-age kids dump into the family stew, parents have little time for work, for play, for each other—even for the kids. It just didn't seem this hectic a generation ago.

Schedule Clutter

"Here in Dallas it's achieve, achieve, achieve," observes Mary Alice Minirth. "Overscheduling, both kids and adults."

How do busy parents avoid neglecting the kids' interests?

"Frank is careful about that," says Mary Alice. "The kids' school holidays are already X-ed off his schedule for next year. Renee's play, for instance. All that. I try to be there all the time, and he's there most of the time. He went with Renee's wilderness trip, canoeing and camping. He takes each of them on a trip to Arkansas at least once a year, and they get to take another friend and her dad.

"He's a workaholic at play too. He works at playing with the kids, and he loves it. They share hobbies—horseback riding, camping, the outdoors.

"But it's hectic. Last week a policeman called to tell us the horses had gotten out. So Frank was out chasing four horses, with the policeman helping. At the same time a litter of kittens was being born in the barn. Renee came screaming up to the house each time a new one appeared. It was an unusual morning.

"We had no vacation at all for the first seven or eight years. Business or some seminar always involved travel. Then it dawned on Frank that it was time to do something besides work. We vacation regularly now. We still talk about Hawaii—how the flowers smelled, how the pineapple tasted. But mostly we go to Arkansas. The kids like that."

Stability Flutter

What children need most of all, though, at any age but particularly during the school years, is a stable family life. Unfortunately, as the kids get wrapped up in school with all their needs and demands, and the parents struggle with work demands, stability tends to flutter.

Family stability is no stronger, no less fluttery than the stability of the marriage itself. Parents who would give their children the best possible schooling, then, should make the marriage their first priority.

There is a retirement benefit to this. Someday your link to the past, your parents, will pass on. Your link to the future, your children, will leave home. In your house will be you and your mate, your marriage the only commitment designed to last a lifetime. It behooves you to keep it strong now, as insurance toward the future.

Both partners must be involved in this complex process of child-raising. It's not just Mom's duty. A child's concept of God is shaped by the earthly father. In fact, there are far more Bible verses addressing fathers than mothers. Again, we recommend *The Father Book*, for more information on the benefit fathers can bring to themselves and their family by being actively involved in childrearing.

We've long known that the child blossoms when its father loves its mother. How can the children learn to express love in a family situation? Include them when picking out Mommy's Valentine gift. Might they plan a special Mother's Day or Father's Day dinner . . . and then help buy the groceries? Encourage them to make place cards for Sunday lunch. Let them help choose the Christmas tree. Children learn love and family unity best by being part of the loving family unit.

"One of the best ways to stop the drifting and make time for each other," says Susan Hemfelt, "is simply to put the children to bed at a decent hour. You'd be amazed how many people don't. The kids, especially little ones, need the sleep. And you and your mate need the time for each other."

That brings up the lock on the bedroom door. Nothing cools ardor faster than a little voice at the door, a child who was supposed to go to sleep and for some reason has risen to haunt you. "*Little* voice?!" A friend of ours laughed. "When the kids were small we laid down the law: Once you're in bed you stay there. No problem. It was when they were grown and coming home from dates or college at all hours that we got the bolt for the bedroom door. If you think a little voice wrecks the romantic mood, try 'Hi, Dad! I'm home! Don't bother to get up; I'll find something to eat in the fridge.' "

If you have school-age children, ask yourself, "Where can we carve out some blocks (possibly small blocks, but blocks nonetheless) of time to nurture our union?"

And, if you have children that can't sleep because of "scary" monsters in their closets or under the bed, we recommend the book: *Things That Go Bump in the Night* by Dr. Paul Warren and Dr. Frank Minirth (Nashville: Thomas Nelson, 1992). Even if your children don't talk about things they're afraid of, it behooves you to explore the methods to properly deal with your children's fears—fear of abandonment, fear of rejection, fear of physical harm, and so on. How you address those fears will have enormous impact on your children's future as functional adults.

Another way you can childproof your marriage is to see and understand how your or your spouse's hidden agendas may be transferring to your children and thus becoming their hidden agendas as well. The only way to do that is to first weed out those hidden agendas of yours.

Chapter 5

Hidden Agendas:
Their Cause and Cure

hen Rosie and Ralph got married, the whole town talked.

"Whatever made her marry him?"

"I simply don't know what he sees in her."

"Isn't that the strangest couple you've ever met?"

It wasn't exactly the kind of talk that makes a bride proud of her catch.

Rosie's mom, also named Rosie, had actually been a riveter during the Second World War. She was never able to live down the good-hearted heckling everyone gave her because of the popular character, "Rosie the Riveter." She had been an industrious lady who raised her children in spite of the father's constant absences. Now Rosie II shared the same sort of reputation for putting in a hard day's work. At five feet ten inches, Rosie II weighed two hundred pounds, and it was all muscle. She worked as a practical nurse in a nursing home, where raw physical strength served her well.

In Ralph, big, boisterous Rosie II picked not so much a mate as a munchkin. Ralph was five feet seven inches tall and weighed fifty pounds less than Rosie. He was going to school. He was always going to school. At twenty-six, he had still not completed his degree in Asian history and religion. Rosie supported him while he studied. It was easy to see why Ralph married hard-working Rosie—three squares a day and a roof over his head, important considerations for a perpetual student. But why did Rosie marry Ralph?

The Power of the Unknown

Picture a London-style double-decker bus. Upstairs, a little kid with a steering wheel sits in the front seat, "driving" merrily. As the bus wallows around a tight right turn the child hauls the wheel to the right. The bus rolls into a traffic circle and the child steers straight ahead. They go around the circle anyway. The kid attempts a left turn but the bus angles right. No matter where the child directs the bus, it will respond to the steering of the hidden driver downstairs. That's what hidden agendas and contracts do to a marriage.

All marriages have unwritten secret contracts and hidden agendas. That is exactly why Passage Two is Passage Two.

Hidden agendas, the fine print of the marriage contract which we never read, does not surface as much during the First Passage. The stars in the newlyweds' eyes obscure hidden agendas even if they do surface. (This, incidentally, really hinders premarital counseling. The couple try their best, but 80 percent of the issues they will face later fail to surface before the wedding.) Now, during and following the Second Passage, is when they tend to appear. The hidden contract may lie dormant for years, only to be triggered by some supposedly random event.

The third task of the Second Passage of marriage is to recognize the hidden contracts in your marriage.

The Third Task: Recognize the Hidden Contracts in Your

Marriage

Rosie got tired of Ralph within three years of the wedding. After all, they had nothing in common. She touted common sense; he dwelt amid dreams and theories. She preferred physical challenges; he played mind games. When they came in for marital counseling, she denied anything could come of it; Ralph was certain counseling would cure the common cold.

Counseling did not cure the common cold, but it certainly revealed important things about their marriage. Rosie and Ralph, like every other couple, entered marriage with two sets of goals, surface agendas and deeper agendas. In counseling, we always work beyond the surface reasons to find what lies underneath.

On the surface, Ralph and Rosie listed these reasons for their marriage:

1. I love her. (I love him.)
2. She is dependable; a woman should be dependable.
3. He is interesting; I want intellectual stimulation, a bright partner.
4. Two can live as cheaply as one.
5. Neither of us is getting any younger, you know.

Their surface contract, then, ostensibly was to find love before they were too old to enjoy it and to marry a person with admirable, desired attributes.

The Unspoken Contract

Delving deep, Dr. Hemfelt uncovered insidious hidden contracts that neither person realized existed. Once the core contract was brought into the open, both of them identified feelings and motivations they had never recognized. Like most people, they found that the simple revelation of what lay hidden brings great relief, a feeling of liberation.

Rosie's was, "I will marry someone who needs my support so much that he won't dare go off and leave me." Remember that Rosie's father abandoned his family for long periods.

Ralph's father had never tasted financial success of any sort. He had exerted intense *but unspoken* pressure upon his children, Ralph especially, to become powerful and wealthy. Ralph's father's unfinished business, his hidden agenda was: "You will take care of me because I never made it myself." That hidden agenda, like every hidden message from parents, filtered down intact to the next generation. But Ralph resisted the pressure so bitterly that he still wasn't earning a living at age twenty-six. His contract: "I will so arrange my life that I will never be able to support my father in the style to which he'd like to become accustomed, and, instead, I will find someone to support me." He married Rosie on that unconscious pretext. While each hidden agenda served its owner, at least in the beginning, both hidden agendas were inimical to the happiness of the spouse. As the marriage matured, the long-range happiness of the couple suffered. Friction grew rapidly once the first bloom of initial love wore off.

Secret Orders

We have found that most hidden contracts remain submerged during the First Passage of marriage. They usually emerge during the Second Passage or later. As illustration, recall the timeworn plot gimmick of films and novels a generation ago. The battleship commander leaves port under sealed orders. He has no idea where he's taking his fleet until he crosses a certain longitude. Then, in a dramatic moment, he opens his sealed orders and learns for the first time of his destination.

Marriage contracts work just like that. The happy couple go steaming off into the sunset unaware where they're *really* going. Then the sealed orders spring into effect and they find themselves on a totally different course. Apparently God allows a lot of unconscious stuff to remain sealed until the marriage gets rolling. After all, if we saw all the thoughts in the darkest corners of our mind, we would become so disillusioned we'd never get together.

Remember Grace and Ron Chevington? How could someone so together and world-wise as Grace pick out a mate like Ron? He was a doormat, a jaded rose to her gilded blossom. During counseling we picked up Grace's hidden agenda. Her family of origin existed on the brink of a civil war due to the constant haranguing between her parents. So affected was she by this childhood of fighting, that she looked for a mate that would not give her any conflict—mellow, easygoing Ron. He bored her to tears within months of their wedding. And, their differences actually enhanced the environment for conflict.

Ralph also illustrates an aspect of hidden contracts. His actual response to a contract was a hundred and eighty degrees different from the unspoken word that had come down from his father.

What About You?

We ask you to look at speed bumps in your marriage. What blips and jolts have interrupted the smooth flow of that first blush of romance? They quite likely represent hidden contracts surfacing. Take a moment to work through the following list of statements. Use them as memory jogs to see if you can spot any hints of hidden agendas in your marriage. Add some more of your own statements at the end of our list.

_____ "I can see a similarity in the way my spouse acts and the way my mother- or father-in-law acts."

_____ "My husband/wife seems to be a direct opposite of his/her mother or father."

_____ "I find myself acting just like my mother or my father in certain instances in our marriage."

_____ "I find myself acting differently than my mother or father just because I want to be different and for no logical reason."

_____ "I sometimes feel that I act a certain way for no apparent reason—like something or someone other than myself is controlling my actions."

_____ "I see the following negative behaviors repeated over and over by my spouse:

_____

_____."

_____ "I find myself repeating the following negative behaviors over and over:

_____

_____."

_____   _____

_____   _____

Repetitious behavior is usually a telltale clue that hidden agendas may be at work.

Repetition

We have found that spouses burdened by an unwholesome hidden marriage contract don't just fulfill it and get it over with. They act it out over and over again, and can't tell you

why. The uglier the hidden agenda—that is, the more dysfunctional it is—the more the couple will find themselves locked
into repeating it.

So we ask you to examine your marriage, seeking out repetitious behavior. If you have ever divorced, look just as closely at
the failed marriage also. What keeps happening over and over
in your life? Is it healthy for you? For your spouse?

Where should you look for repetition that signals deeper
problems?

Your Sexual Life.

Do situations or occurrences rob you of satisfaction or orgasm? All couples have their good times and not-so-good
times. Rather, look for a frequently recurring problem.

For instance, a husband might realize that whenever he initi-
ates sex, he hears the same refrain from his wife, "That's all you
ever think about. That's all you ever value in our relationship."
In some marriages the wife may be right: The husband is too
aggressive. In others, however, the wife may be repeating an
old message that she unconsciously picked up from her parents.
Even if the wife does yield to the husband's advances, he may
still be frustrated because he constantly feels chastised about his
male sexuality.

Think about the following recurrent problems we hear from
clients in our counsel. Add some more of your own. They may
indicate repetitious behavior which alludes to hidden agendas
at work.

_____ You find yourself robbed of sexual orgasm because of
          intruding thoughts. It happens frequently during your
          sexual encounters.

_____ You have not experienced satisfaction with your sexual
          relationship for a long time. Instead of looking for-
          ward to sex with your spouse, you actually dread it.

_____ Once you were married, sex lost its excitement and
          vitality. Your sexual experiences are routine and pre-
          dictable.

_____ _____

_____ _____

Obviously, we are all individuals and as individuals we experience our sexual relationships differently. Problems in the sexual arena of a marriage can be very complex, which is why we devote the entire next chapter to this subject alone. What we're looking for here, though, is repetitious behavior that happens in your sexual relationship, especially repetitious behavior that may be a hidden echo of Mom's or Dad's attitude toward their own sexuality, behavior that might point to underlying issues. Another repetitious behavior we examine is emotions.

Your Emotional Life.

Do your spouse's actions or attitudes consistently frustrate you? Turn you off? Alienate you? Anger you?

For instance, does your spouse seem to be constantly overreacting to situations? Do you feel as if you are always walking through a mine field, never knowing what will set your spouse off?

Look over the following list to see if any of these behaviors sound familiar.

_____ "I can't criticize or mention something that bothers me about my spouse's actions without him/her exploding at me and saying all I ever do is nag, nag, nag."

_____ "Every time I ask my mate to do something, he/she acts as if I am taking advantage of him/her."

_____ "I have to 'tiptoe' around my spouse, catering to his/her needs, or experience the explosion of anger or tears from my mate."

Now list three things you did recently that upset your spouse:

1. _____
2. _____
3. _____

Are these things similar in any way? If each of these things is related in some unusual way to your spouse's explosive reactions, what's the pattern?

For example, with Rosie and Ralph, Ralph had to tread very lightly around Rosie. It seemed nothing he did was right in her eyes. Rosie had a volatile temper and would use it on Ralph, pointing out his weaknesses.

Through counseling we got Ralph to see a pattern to Rosie's anger. Every time he tried something, something that would make him more independent, like travel, she would harp on the negative aspects: "You can't even pack your own suitcase, how do you expect to board a plane without me?"

That kind of negative reinforcement only tipped Ralph over more on the dependency side—which was exactly what Rosie secretly wanted. She didn't want Ralph to leave her as her father left her mother.

Now, what's the pattern you may see with your spouse's emotional responses?

The pattern I see is _____

_____

_____.

Now The Other Way Around.

What about your emotional response to your spouse? Are there any things you find you do over and over because of your spouse's actions? Do any of the following sound familiar?

_____ "My spouse is helpless with the kids. She/he can't change a diaper properly, feed them, or even get them into bed when I'm gone. It just irritates me that he/she can't do anything right where the kids are concerned."

_____ "It just figures. I give the checkbook to _____ and he/she screws it up. I'm the only one that's capable of handling our finances."

List three things your spouse did recently that upset you:

1. _____

2. _____

3. _____

Are these things similar in any way? Repetitive? If each of these things is related in some unusual way to your angry reactions, what's the pattern?

The pattern for our statements above would be that this person is reluctant to release control—the children and money matters for two examples. He/she probably finds fault with everything his/her spouse does to participate in other family responsibilities. That's the pattern to look for: anger or emotional responses over similar incidents. What's the pattern that you can see in the three things you listed above?

The pattern I see is _____

_____.

An explosive spouse may be unconsciously responding to a parent who overcontrolled him or her. If your spouse had to claw to hold his or her turf in childhood, that pattern will be repeated in your relationship.

Think about the patterns you identified as we walk through the process of dealing with hidden marriage contracts. These patterns are the first clues to unraveling submerged hidden agendas. You don't consciously know your hidden agenda, but your subconscious does and it acts it out through repetitious behavior.

Digging Up Those Buried Motives

"It's absolutely hopeless!" Ian, a transplanted Australian, sat in our office scowling. "I suppose it's wrong, but what'll I do? Live in a monastery the rest of my life?"

"I guess I don't blame him, and it hurts me terribly when I find out, but I can't help it." His wife, Rhoda, blonde and doe-eyed, perched elegantly on the edge of the other overstuffed chair. "I have to agree with Ian. It's hopeless. I just can't see any way out. The only reason we're in here is because my parents want us to try counseling before we file for divorce."

"It's merely motions you're going through. Right?"

Rhoda looked at Ian. She appeared almost ready to cry. "I suppose you could say that, yes."

We see this constantly in counseling and in life outside the clinic: people in quiet desperation, devoid of hope. "If your marriage were turned around and the reasons for your problems brought to light, would you make the effort needed to save it?"

Ian shook his head. "I can't see that happening."

"We know that. Would you?"

Ian and Rhoda both pondered the question a moment before responding, weighing the possible consequences—always a good sign. Both were hesitant but both said yes.

We could begin.

What we would do for Rhoda and Ian's marriage, which was very, very sick, are the same things that you can do to improve an already healthy marriage. The principles remain the same; the differences are one of degree.

In clinic work we begin by assuming people in all marriages try to get their needs met, carve out an identity, and establish some sort of lasting security. Their attempts at this may be extremely dysfunctional, damaging to themselves and to the relationship, but the attempts are genuine, nonetheless. When the relationship *really* gets complicated is when each person tries consciously to fulfill these goals in one way, and still pursues the same goals, based on the hidden agendas, in another way at an unconscious level. It's like trying to play chess on two boards at once; you never know where the next piece is coming from.

For example, a man seeks to meet his sexual needs. At the conscious level, he's trying to be a good lover, so that his spouse will respond as a good lover. But his unconscious program is saying, "All women are shrews; don't get too close." He has the best of intentions, but it's not working right because he doesn't know what's going on with that second chessboard.

First Examine the Symptoms

Ian came to the United States on a scholarship, studying agriculture at Colorado State University. When he left Australia, his mates ragged him good-naturedly about all the sexy, pushy American women he'd have to fend off. Imagine his surprise when he actually met one. She was movie-star pretty, bold and brassy, and promiscuous. Rhoda.

They became sexually involved almost immediately. Charmed by his manners and accent, she married him after a two-month courtship. Two years later, she had shut down sexually altogether and had recently discovered Ian in his third extramarital affair . . . that she knew about. He refused to discuss the possibility of others. The roles had somehow reversed. Prior to marriage he had remained monogamous; she flitted about. Now she had turned off to sex even in the marriage bed and he roamed freely.

You can gauge the amount of unfinished business by the amount and intensity of a spouse's hidden contracts. Two people at war, or at quiet war, indicate that major issues were not worked out between the hidden and spoken contracts. We more or less tune out the presenting symptoms; they're only a guide to what's happening underneath; and look for underlying causes. "What are the hidden contracts here that aren't out on the table?" we ask ourselves.

How could a marriage with Ian and Rhoda's shattering sexual problems be mended? We began with an inventory of their parents' and grandparents' possible hidden contracts.

Inventorying Prior Generations

We usually find hidden agendas in the form of time-release capsules. Time-release capsules, you'll remember, are those insidious beads that lie latent within our psyche, waiting to trigger into action. Much like the beads in a cold capsule that kick in throughout a twelve-hour period for relief of cold symptoms, time-release capsules from our past (our parents' and our grandparents' marriages) lie dormant, waiting to kick in and affect our current marriage. If not recognized and resolved in our generation, these time-triggered issues will pass to our children's generation and so on, until they are dealt with.

Many times these time-release capsules kick in through sexual expression. Sexual expression is usually just the camouflage for deeper unresolved issues from prior generations, such as unfulfilled dreams, financial failures, and fractured personal relationships. This was the case in Ian and Rhoda's marriage.

Sexual Expression

"Ian," we asked, "if you could put into words your parents' attitudes toward sex, what would they be?"

"Haven't a clue. Never talked to them about it."

"No facts-of-life discussion?"

"Not really. They thought I knew more than I did." He snorted. "So did I."

We asked Ian to assess such things as how he felt as a child when both parents were in the same room: safe? comfortable? on edge? wanting to leave the room? Was there peace or tension? Did the parents fight much? About what? Did Dad go out often or stay out late? How about Mum? How did Mum and Dad respond when a member of the extended family died? How, if at all, did they express grief?

We asked the same sorts of things about the grandparents, both sides, as much as he could remember. He remembered his older cousins discussing openly that his grandfather catted around. At the time, he had no idea what that meant. His father went down to the pub nearly every night, but then most of the men in Blackall, Australia did that. His mother liked to read romance novels after the kids went to bed.

His grandfather, a gas station operator, enjoyed moderate financial success, and maintained a steady income even though the farm-based economy of the area fluctuated wildly. Neither parents nor grandparents ever mentioned a word about grief or intimacy.

Rhoda's turn.

"Tell us what you remember about your grandparents as a couple."

"Let's see. My mom's mother was the youngest. She stayed home, single, and took care of Great-grandma. She was twenty-six when Great-grandma finally died, and she really cut loose. From sitting at home with a crabby old woman every night, to never coming home at night. Freedom, you know?"

"Then she met and married your grandfather."

"Yeah. When Mom was growing up, Grandma used to mention her past sometimes. It embarrassed Mom to death."

"Embarrassed, or shamed?"

"Shamed would be a better word. Right."

"How did your grandfather respond to that?"

"Don't know. He knew what she was like when he married her. I suppose he made peace with all that."

Rhoda's mom and dad certainly never made peace sexually. Rhoda dredged through her memories, seeking unspoken messages her mother may have delivered. From random comments her mother made just prior to Rhoda's wedding, Rhoda sensed (though it was not said directly) that her mother considered marital sex evil and a burden.

"Reflect on how your parents express feelings toward each other. Do they seem comfortable together? Affectionate?"

Rhoda thought about that a moment. "Civil, nice to each other but not what I'd call affectionate." She stared at the wall. Her face softened. "Of course! It was right in front of me all the time. The last five years I was home, they slept in separate bedrooms. They still do. Mom says he tosses and turns too much."

Regarding other aspects of the parents' and grandparents' lives and attitudes, Ian and Rhoda engaged in part guesswork and part detective work. Like figuring out who-done-it in a classic mystery novel, they pieced together fragments of what they knew to make a picture.

"My dad had a master's degree in business," Ian recalled, "but he never got above clerking. Never owned or managed anything. Grandpapa never gave the petrol station to him; that went to the older brother. Uncle James. Good old Uncle James was perfect, to hear Grandpapa talk."

"What was your father's reputation in that small town?" we asked.

Ian burst out laughing, but it wasn't humor. It was pain. "A joke. Cheap wine and shady ladies."

"Not too good, then?" we asked.

"No. Dad never really achieved any financial security," Ian mused. "Do you suppose I'm trying too hard because of that?"

"The anomaly, if you'd call it that," we agreed, "indicates something going on. That sort of incongruity often tells something."

How About You?

If, like Ian and Rhoda, you see a need for change in the area of sexual expression, you will be tempted to pay attention only to that aspect of your family's past. Go beyond that, uncover what this really camouflages. Regardless of your speed bumps, explore every area where hidden agendas lurk, including attitudes toward death and saying good-bye.

Here as well, a dual-answer workbook approach, such as that used in *Getting Ready for Marriage Workbook* by Jerry D. Hardin and Dianne C. Sloan (Nashville: Thomas Nelson, 1992), can reveal much about your sexual shortcomings and longings, as well as those of your parents. Trying to reflect the influences you feel shape your attitudes and pleasures regarding sex, check the statements below that apply to you:

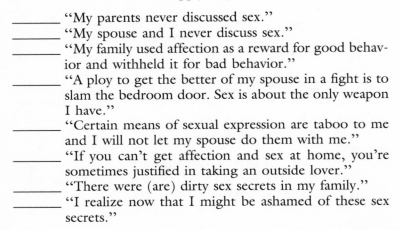

_____ "My parents never discussed sex."

_____ "My spouse and I never discuss sex."

_____ "My family used affection as a reward for good behavior and withheld it for bad behavior."

_____ "A ploy to get the better of my spouse in a fight is to slam the bedroom door. Sex is about the only weapon I have."

_____ "Certain means of sexual expression are taboo to me and I will not let my spouse do them with me."

_____ "If you can't get affection and sex at home, you're sometimes justified in taking an outside lover."

_____ "There were (are) dirty sex secrets in my family."

_____ "I realize now that I might be ashamed of these sex secrets."

Do you see any relationship between your parents' attitudes and your own from the various statements? As Ian and Rhoda worked all this out they had to keep repeating to themselves, "This is no time for secrets." They were exploring roots, hidden threads, and that meant uncovering some dirt if need be. They reported feeling a mix of titillation and dread as they began honestly to look at their sexual views and mores for the first time.

What Do You Need to Deal With?

So, like Ian, you see abnormality, something that just doesn't ring right. What do you do about it?

Ian shook his head. "Nah! You got kangaroos in your top paddock. You're saying just 'cause Mum would catch my father in the dunny knocking back Africa Speaks. . ."

We interrupted. "Pardon?"

"Sorry." Ian grinned, but the smile faded quickly. "I think you're crazy. You say just because Mum would now and then find him hiding in the privy out back, sneaking a drink of cheap red wine . . . Africa Speaks is this awful stuff . . . he didn't have a business head . . . couldn't make a fair go of it. . . . Anyway, I can't see how that's affecting what I do on another continent. I like the ladies because I get nothing at home. Believe me, I didn't get married so I could spend years without . . . you know." He grimaced, shamefaced. "It's Rhoda. Talk to her."

"You're half of the marriage. We'll ask both of you. What can you see that was left undone in your parents' and grandparents' generations? What did they fail to deal with? What need did that leave lacking in you?"

Rhoda and Ian worked on that for a week, sorting out details. The answers they came up with: Guilt. Shame. Failure—business failure and failure to establish comfortable sexual relationships in marriage.

"Comfortable sexual relationship in marriage?" Rhoda shook her head during our next session. "Neither Ian nor I have our act together on that one. But we can't fix the past. We can't go back and change our parents' lives."

"True. Ian, with your background you can appreciate this. Picture a series of pastures with gates between them."

"Paddocks."

"Right. When all the gates are open you can introduce live-stock at one end and run them clear through all the paddocks to the other end."

Ian grinned. "Don't tell me you forgot to close gates when you were little too."

"Ah, so it's personal for you. Good. And that's exactly how you stop the sheep or cattle. Close the gate. The distant paddocks are your ancestors. The third one back there is your grandparents. The one next to you is your parents. You're the paddock right here and beyond you, the gate wide open, is the paddock that will be your children."

"The different generations?"

"Exactly. Now let's say you want to grow flowers in your paddock. Intimacy and romance are often symbolized as flowers."

"Not with sheep running through you won't. They'd eat 'em to the ground." Ian's face lit up. "I see! These problems, this unfinished business you call it, are the sheep: the shame and guilt and failure. They destroy the love."

"Exactly. The sheep roamed from your grandparents' pastures and your parents' to your own. If you don't see them and stop them, and close the gates, they'll continue on to your children's."

Ian nodded. "Tell me how to get them out of my paddock."

"You can't get rid of them if you don't notice they're there. You just did that. Once you've identified them, you can control them. By grieving them and the damage they did to your parents, your grandparents, and you, you close the gates. In fact, some therapists refer to the process as 'closure.' "

Ian never imagined that his parents' or grandparents' marriages could have any impact on his struggles with Rhoda.

The sheep in your own pastures have caused problems, for others and for you. They may not have been dealt with in prior generations, so it is most appropriate to go ahead and grieve them in this generation. The grieving process, generally well known, is dealt with in detail in other works. In our counseling we try to help patients deal with the losses of their lives by grieving them through.

Learning how to grieve is essential in a fallen world. Grieving losses is important in your journey through the passages of marriage. We showed Ian and Rhoda how to grieve through the issues they discovered in their marriage. Let's work through the process of grief now.

Think of a recent occasion in your marriage when you felt hurt or wronged. If you can, use an incident where the wound is still open. The incident does not specifically have to be between you and your spouse. Perhaps you had to place your aging parent in a retirement home. Identify that incident as IT as we move through the stages of grief in the next section.

Shock and Denial

When we asked Ian if he knew his parents' attitudes toward sex, he replied, "Haven't a clue!" Yet, with a little probing he could remember that his father went to the pub nearly every night and his grandfather catted around.

Think about the way IT startled you at the very first—the shock and disbelief. "That didn't really happen!" "It can't be!" The shock of your incident might have lasted for a fleeting second or for a longer time. People who hang up right here at the beginning of grief walk about, literally, in a daze that can last for years. That often happens, if the trauma is great or the loss severe. Recognize the shock and denial that comes with learning something unsavory or depressing.

Depression

The word *depress* actually means "to push down." Even though we experience depression as pain, it's really an emotional numbness as the definition suggests. We push down and shut down our feelings. Patients often express depression as the world becoming gray, as if the tube on the color television is broken and you're back to the old black-and-white picture. Everything loses color and vibrancy.

People naturally react to depression as Rhoda did. They try anything to get the color back. Rhoda was actually forcing herself to feel again by acting out sexually. Unconsciously she was saying to herself, *Maybe I can feel love and closeness if I enter into these intimate relationships. Maybe this one will do it.*

Do you feel numb? If so, are you trying to jump start your feelings? Recognize that as part of the depression.

If IT is on the magnitude of the loss of a minor business deal, depression is no big deal. But if IT is the parent you put in a home or a move to another state, far away from your family and friends, the depression can last for months or years. Depression is an expected and necessary part of the process. Do you recall the depression that accompanied some other major loss in your life?

Expect depression. This is a heavy load you're dealing with. It will weigh you down. Fear not; the depression is almost always temporary.

Bargaining or Magical Thinking

There is a period when you'll seek some way out. We call it bargaining and magical thinking. You might try to cut a deal with God or another human being, perhaps with your spouse or parents.

"Okay, God," you might say. "Get me out of this depression and I'll tithe 12 percent."

"If only I can justify the loss, I won't have to grieve it. The pain will go away." "If only." "If you will but . . ." What bargains or "if onlys" came to your mind when IT happened?

Rhoda was trying to strike a bargain with God. Even though she thought she believed in premarital sex, she instinctively felt ashamed of her actions (we often find this to be true, by the way). She also carried her mother's shame about grandma's wild oats. Her bargain with God?

"I'll pay the price. I'll be nonsexual in this marriage for a month or a year or a decade—or the balance of this relationship." Unconsciously she was doing penance or wearing that scarlet letter of Nathaniel Hawthorne's heroine.

Unfortunately it's natural for us to believe in bargaining and magical thinking. Are you promising to do x, y, or z to pay the price for this situation in your life? Eventually you must put the magic and bargaining away. They don't work anyway.

Sadness

Sadness is what most people think of when they think of grieving, but it is only one part—this fifth part—of the process. And you can't experience true grief if you haven't really worked through the earlier steps.

Unfortunately people try to go directly to sadness in grieving. In counseling they'll indirectly say to us, "Let me be sad for the next hour and get this out of the way." It's the way of our vending machine-oriented society. Put a quarter in and get instant gratification, resolution of the problem, plopping into the bin. Before you can experience true grief, however, you must have overcome your denial and bargaining and your depression. Rhoda had to give herself permission to be angry at grandma for her childish overreaction to caring for her elderly grandmother; Rhoda had to be angry at her mom for talking about the shame she felt; and Rhoda had to be angry that she grew up in a family where the women were not given a healthy attitude toward sex.

Then Rhoda could get to true grief, crying for all the losses in her grandmother and mother's lives, the losses in Rhoda's own childhood and her premarital relationships, and those of the last two years in a barren marriage.

Now it's your turn. Recount the sorrow IT generated. Do

you remember it? Memories of sorrow fade; that is one of the nicest things about sadness.

Forgiveness and Resolution

Forgiveness, acceptance, and resolution complete the process. Be aware that you cannot reach them either without going through the other stages first. Cheap forgiveness and casual acceptance solve nothing.

Once Rhoda was able to grieve her losses, she was able to forgive her grandmother, her mother, and herself. Counselors sometimes talk about secondary virginity or sexual rebirth. If a person truly forgives herself, then she can feel emotionally and spiritually pure. Virginity is more a state of the heart, we've found, than of the hymen, especially for those who have been sexually abused or who have misused premarital sex.

Just who needs be forgiven in regard to IT? What is your part in that forgiveness? You must also forgive yourself if that is appropriate, you know. Forgiveness is so important and integral to any marriage, we will devote a chapter to it later. For now, determine what forgiveness is necessary regarding IT, and detail how you should go about it.

Are other steps necessary before IT is resolved comfortably and satisfactorily? A bandage on a cut finger or a letter to restore a friendship—so many incidents require careful resolution. Mending such bridges always pays immense dividends, to yourself and to others.

Having dealt with past layers of problems by grieving them through, you have another task to complete in regard to them. Use them to ferret out what sort of hidden agenda they might have engendered in you.

After reviewing the history of both Rhoda's and Ian's relatives, we posed this question: "Rhoda, it's safe to assume your mother is acting, probably unconsciously, on her own hidden contract when she seeks a separate bedroom or displays little affection. It's also a safe assumption you picked up some form of that attitude. How might you have translated it into your own hidden contract?"

She didn't come up with the answer immediately. It took time. Eventually, she realized what her innermost self was saying: "I'm ashamed. I'm going to create a sexless marriage."

"Ian? What about you?"

"I suppose," he ventured, "something about 'It's all right to have sex outside marriage.' I grew up hearing the church, and even my mum, saying it's wrong. My mind says it's wrong, but that's not my mind talking, right? I can see now how I got the word from my father and his father, and they never said a thing."

Ian and Rhoda came to understand how each was wrong in the relationship. They asked God and each other for forgiveness. Ian broke off the extramarital sexual relationships and committed to being faithful to Rhoda, no matter what. Rhoda chose not to withhold sex from Ian, and instead to talk to him about her anger and fears. Together, they formed a new hope for their marriage.

This process was not easy for both of them. And, one of the biggest items they had to face was their sexual problems.

Chapter 6

What to Do with All That Sexual Baggage

*F*rom her nest beneath the covers, Grace Chevington watched her husband prepare for bed. Just like always, Ron dropped his drawers as if modesty were a thing of the '40s. He made such a big deal out of his handsome face and trim physique, but his physique was beginning to be untrim in a few key places.

He glanced at her and grimaced. "You've changed, Grace."

"How?"

"You no longer try to hide your disdain when you look at me. It used to be, you'd at least keep the disgusted frown off your face."

"Really." She felt her face twisting into a smirk. "Ironic. So they're both obvious now—my disgust and your love handles."

For Grace and Ron, the honeymoon was over. Second Passage reality had landed on them like a haybale on a Twinkie. Lovemaking for them had become mechanical, predictable. It occurred once or twice a month at most. By their fourth anniversary Grace was considering separate bedrooms.

What was happening to Grace and Ron happens to all too many couples as they traverse the treacherous Second Passage. Physically, they were as capable of pleasure as any newlywed. The problems came from within, from that underrated sex organ, the brain. Let's look at some of the mind's tricks and at the challenges that overcome them.

The Major Challenge: Shed the Sexual
Baggage of the Past

Picture newlyweds arriving at their new home with half a dozen suitcases and an overnight bag or two. The first day, they may simply enjoy their union without unpacking much. The way to unpack, of course, is to open the suitcases out on the floor one by one and remove what is needed. Picture, though, the way couples of the First and Second Passage (and often subsequent passages as well) actually do it; they haul the suitcases right into bed with them. Try to enjoy intimacy with those suitcases stacked all over the bed, taking up room. Like all good baggage, these suitcases are tagged and identified.

Tag: The Myths Couples Bring from the Past

A lot of fiction embellishes the fact of sexual union, and it can damage or delay sexual satisfaction. For example, Ron had always heard, "A good spouse never says no." He feared his masculinity might come into question if he didn't perform on demand. Women fall prey to the myth as well. Because of it, many women fear that if he doesn't get sex here whenever he wants it, he'll seek it elsewhere.

"A woman's only good response is a passive one. Just lie there and let him have his way." In counseling we find women whose hearts are firmly convinced of the myth that good girls must remain passive. Unless counterproductive forces are at work, discussion and self-talk can convince these women that it is both normal and moral for the woman to initiate sexual activity and to participate fully.

A lot of misinformation centers around orgasm. "It's my spouse's fault if I don't have one." Maybe it is, but don't bet the ranch on it. Probably what you both need is more openness in talking about it. A man might decide a woman is incapable of it anyway, so why try. Another couple might feel that if the performance isn't athletic, it's not erotic. The man who falls victim to one or two episodes of impotence might quit trying altogether.

And then there are the romance novels, and the cinema, and the sheets-and-bare-shoulders TV movies. "Oh, wow, that's exciting and fulfilling and dramatic! How come we're so clumsy and awkward? Why isn't it the singing, zinging thing the novelists describe?" Keep in mind that good sex, like good golf, takes practice. Also remember that the media are not training sources; they are fantasy machines. They project a larger-than-life view of sex in order to promote the fantasy. They want to leave you breathless and wide-eyed, not better informed. The cops and robbers don't shoot real bullets in those movies, either. It's an elaborately staged set-up. Your love life is the real thing and, pursued with elan, will provide infinitely better pleasure and intimacy than any manufactured fantasy.

Tag: Sexual Taboos

Possibly the most common dysfunctions a couple must combat are the sexual taboos they learned in childhood. These are the deep-seated precepts, such as, "It's wrong to be sexual inside a family." "Sex is dirty." These taboos enter the couple's life when they first marry and become a family, or especially after the first child is born, for then the marriage unit truly is a family.

Grace and Ron shared an unconscious message, an equation: Sexy = illicit.

And the reverse also thus appeared as true: Illicit = sexy.

Therefore, if I'm sexy, I'm being illicit or dirty or immoral.

In some couples we counsel, one or both of them may experience physical problems with intercourse or their emotional satisfaction freezes up.

During that big trend when couples were living together, another sexual taboo we call the incest inhibition wreaked havoc. Couples would apparently do well with several years of living together. Confident that they were compatible, they would formalize the union, then divorce in a few months or a year. The incest inhibition that said, "It is wrong to have sex within a family" had remained silently buried until the couple said the normal "I do's" and actually became a family.

Grace and Ron were sexually united for nearly two years before they married. But as soon as they married—in fact, within
days of the ceremony—Grace simply shut down. Desire fled.
Sex had become domestic. And yet, because married couples
are supposed to be sexual and the precept is buried too deeply
to find, sex went on, muted by the conundrum. She hated it.
Finally, Ron quit bothering her (his words, tinged with sadness).

Ron had his own set of problems. For him as well as Grace,
premarital sex was far more satisfying than any they experienced
in marriage. It was a function of that sex-is-dirty attitude. Since
sex outside the union is perceived as wrong, the sex-is-dirty
feeling is strongly reinforced. Suddenly, the couple say a few
wedding words, throw a whiz-bang reception, and sex isn't
dirty anymore. The head can make the switch, but the heart
gets thrown for a loop.

Tag: Sexual Abuse, Particularly in Childhood

We have never yet seen an exception to the rule that a man or
woman abused in childhood will suffer some degree of sexual
dysfunction in adulthood. Problems within the person include
damage done by sexual abuse and other traumatic sexual experiences. Such damage affects marital sex. In these cases professional counseling is almost always necessary. We also recommend the book, *The Wounded Heart,* by Dr. Dan Allendar
(Colorado Springs: NavPress, 1990).

Not all sexual abuse is the dramatic sort that newspapers
dwell upon. It can be very subtle and still cause lasting damage.
Edith Hawkes learned that.

Edith came in for counsel regarding sexual dysfunction.
More properly speaking, Edith's husband dragged her in. She
didn't see that it was much of a problem. He was going nuts
with her quirks.

Edith had a modesty fetish, as her husband phrased it. She
could not bear to let him see her any way other than fully
clothed. When they first married, everything was grand except
for one little kink; any time Edith's husband saw her undress,
or asked her to undress, or looked at her, she would become
extremely uncomfortable and have to cover up. They made
love in total darkness. He dismissed it at first, chalking it off to

shyness in the new union. But her problem intensified, and by the Second Passage of marriage, despite the birth of three children, she wore a heavy robe to bed. She could not tolerate his looking at her.

"You feel uncomfortable now. What feelings made you uncomfortable when you were young?" We started at the beginning and moved forward through Edith's life, exploring feelings and events. Her father had never sexually molested her or ever touched her wrongly or made unseemly remarks. But every now and then she'd catch Dad staring at her. His look made her squirm even now as she described it. Yet it wasn't actually leering. Repeatedly, Dad would burst into the bathroom or bedroom without knocking, catching her in states of semi-undress. There was always some legitimate reason; at least, he always had an excuse. After all, he was her father. Even though there was no episode of molestation, Dad's interest was inappropriate and she sensed it even in childhood. Recognizing and grieving that covert abuse helped her master her inhibition.

Tag: Abortion

Sally and Steve Pauling had no problems being mutual friends. They could find no significant problems in their past. Their families of origin both seemed to treat sexuality in healthy ways. And yet, Sally could not derive pleasure from intimacy. She had turned off to sex completely.

The nitty-gritty of Sally and Steve Pauling's problems emerged in the third session. We were talking about children when Sally blurted out, "We'd have a baby now if we didn't . . . never mind."

Alerted, we explored what that sentence had left unspoken. Sally and Steve both grew up with conservative religious beliefs that forbade sexual relations outside marriage. Despite that, they became physically intimate some months before their wedding. Sally got pregnant. Steve, unwilling and unable to deal with fatherhood at this stage in his life, encouraged Sally to have an abortion. At the time, it seemed the only way out. After all, it was perfectly legal. Had the baby come to term, it would have been born the week they entered counseling.

Here was the main issue, buried beneath unrelated issues. Steve had refused at the time to discuss what they were doing or to talk about it after it was done. When Sally desperately wanted his support, he considered the matter finished. With counseling, she came to understand her intense resentment toward Steve, that he had not been there for her emotionally when she needed him most. She finally saw that her sexual shutdown was her only weapon, a sexual weapon, to express her resentment and punish him for his apparent coldness.

An abortion in a woman's past will sometimes cause disruption in sexual intimacy. It's supposed to be over with, done. The wedding was going to take care of it, but the issue remains. Usually, he doesn't appreciate what the woman is going through and forgets about it, failing to recognize the intensity of her feelings. She expects him to share her grief and sense of guilt when he doesn't even recognize it as a baby. Conflict results.

We know from our practices and our personal lives, that if married persons do not resolve the special problems generated by an abortion in the past, they separate right in the beginning, emotionally if not residentially. They don't trust each other. They are hurting. The man feels threatened and the woman is carrying all the load. As we mentioned, the husband usually doesn't want to admit it was a baby. That leaves the woman to handle all the emotional, psychological, and physical trauma for both of them. Typically, he won't talk about it; threatened by her anger, he may not listen if she tries to talk about it, or he thrusts it aside. Frequently, he's reluctant to deal with the mistake at all. So he is not open to sharing what the woman is going through. It becomes a formidable barrier to intimacy and a bar to any further movement through the passages.

The first thing we do when counseling couples with an abortion in their past is to help them resolve the responsibility fifty-fifty. Then we can lead the couple into mutual grieving and mutual forgiveness. It sounds simple, easy, even glib. In reality, it is immensely difficult and painful. It takes time.

Tag: Biological Problems

Still another source of relationship problems sometimes makes itself known about now: infertility. When a couple decide they want children, nothing may happen except an increase in anxiety and doubt. Sex becomes a mechanical exercise to meet a stated goal, nothing else. The man feels used. He may even go through all sorts of unpleasant medical procedures. So may the woman. Only, she is thoroughly preoccupied with becoming pregnant. She neither feels very sexy nor comes across as such.

What else can affect a couple's sexual relationship, what other tags?

Tag: Unresolved Conflict

Problems will be generated by the marital relationship itself where anger, frustration, and resentment reside. "Conflict and lack of communication are frequent reasons for dysfunction," Debi explains. "Below the conscious level, the person yearns to get back at the spouse for real or perceived faults and slights. He or she uses sex as a tool. Often the person simply cannot perform and may not consciously know why. Withholding sex and pleasure is perhaps the only weapon that person has."

Such was the case with Steve and Sally. Unconsciously, she resented his emotional abandonment through the abortion. The only way to get back at him was to use sex as a means for punishing him for his apparent coldness. She saw finally that her sexual shutdown was her weapon against Steve.

If you harbor resentment or bitterness, your sexual activity will suffer, one way or another.

Sex, we have found, mirrors the marriage's general health. When heavy problems and lasting dysfunctions persist, the sexual life suffers. The husband says, "If things went better in bed, everything would be all right," even as the wife says, "If we had our financial affairs in order, sex would be a lot better."

Any stressor shoving at your marriage right now can affect your sexual intimacy. Yet we don't want to suggest that every slight irregularity reflects a sexual problem. During the first two years of marriage a great deal of sexual adjustment takes place. It is not at all uncommon for couples to go through phases when they shut down. They may go overboard for a few weeks and then go dormant for a few more. As a short-term dysfunction it's not really a dysfunction. They're working out a rhythm. When problems persist, into this Second Passage and beyond, though, and cannot be talked through, we urge professional counseling.

Tag: *Personal Problems*

Not all personal problems within and between the spouses are related to sexual taboos and time-release bombs from the past. Each human being possesses a finite amount of emotional energy with which to deal with life, just as that person also possesses a finite amount of physical energy. They are two different kinds of energy. Consider marathon runners. They are in much better shape than most desk-bound folk, with the stamina to run over two dozen miles. For the first part of the race they all are putting out about the same amount of effort and spending the same amount of energy. As the miles drag on and on, the race reveals that some have more energy to expend than others. They go the distance and they get there faster. All who cross the finish line are elated at having completed the course. Their emotional energy is high even though physically they are totally drained.

Similarly, when a marriage partner invests a great deal of emotional energy in one area, another area may suffer. The woman who has just completed a marathon is in no shape to go home and clean house that day. The woman who has just put in an eight-hour or longer day at the office and has had to cook dinner, put the kids to bed, and straighten the house has no energy, physical or emotional, for sex. The best she can do is collapse in bed for some sleep. The same for the man if he is responsible for these jobs.

A marriage partner may have very little physical stress in life and may expend very small amounts of available physical energy. That person can be exhausted, nonetheless—exhausted emotionally.

Grace Chevington had been watching her elderly mother grow more feeble. The mother steadfastly refused to enter an assisted living arrangement, and Grace lived eight hundred miles away, unable to help. Like a marathon runner, Grace was investing an immense amount of emotional energy in worry, financial concerns, indecision about what to do. Because she did not have a limitless supply of that energy, some other emotional investments went begging. Ron claimed she was a cold fish. She wasn't cold. She was utterly spent.

Arguments, divisions, prolonged friction, fear, nagging irritations, financial concerns, personal losses and tragedies, and other negatives all take a huge toll on emotional energy. They therefore affect the sexual union in a negative way.

And yes, the opposite also holds true. Positive emotional energy—love, enthusiasm for life—can have a positive effect on sexual intimacy.

For more on this subject we recommend the book, *Worry-Free Living* by Dr. Frank Minirth, Dr. Paul Meier, and Don Hawkins (Nashville: Thomas Nelson, 1989).

Dumping the Baggage

How does one shove all those suitcases out of the bed? Grace and Ron had a bunch of luggage to get rid of. Every time they tried to simply sit down and talk, they found themselves screaming at each other (a trained on-air voice can really enunciate when it yells, too). At four and a half years of marriage, and eager to dissolve this sour union, Grace and Ron ended up in counseling.

Before she met Ron, Grace dated a couple of guys who wouldn't take no for an answer. She didn't realize it at the time, but that's abuse—date rape—and it took its toll. But there was more affecting their relationship. We already alluded to the problems sexual taboos and other baggage from the past caused them. They had no idea where their attitudes and problems were coming from.

So for starters, we went back through their personal histories to explore both stated and unspoken messages. Grace and Ron talked, and talked, and talked to us. Because they were in joint counseling, each heard stories of the other's past that they had never heard before. This in itself improved their intimacy, as each came to know and appreciate the other better.

Grace's parents had slept in separate rooms for many years. As a child growing up, Grace did not consciously understand the significance of that, but her subconscious grasped the message: "It's wrong to be sexual inside a family."

Every time she went out during her dating years, her mother warned her not to get pregnant. "It's wrong to be sexual" was that message. Mom never bothered to temper her admonitions with healthy messages about appropriate sex.

We dealt with her sexual taboos, bringing them to the surface and replacing them with the correct message that sex in a marriage is legitimate, that sex is the God-given means of union between man and wife. Her inhibitions melted slowly, bit by bit. The new message was something she had always known in her head. But the silent hidden message shouted down that head knowledge.

What About You?

Analyze your parents' lifestyle carefully. Analyze your grandparents' also, if you're familiar at all with it. Here are a few of the statements from *Getting Ready for Marriage Workbook* we mentioned before. Check those that apply to your family of origin:

_____ "In my family, sex was not discussed."

_____ "My mother and father hugged and kissed in front of the children."

_____ "My parents slept in separate beds."

_____ "My parents believed that a marriage should be faithful and permanent."

_____ "My mother thought intercourse was a wife's duty."

_____ "I received excellent sexual information from my parents."

_____ "I never felt free to ask my parents anything about sexual issues."

Look back at the statements you checked on your family-of-origin's sexual attitudes. Are there any actions or attitudes in your childhood that might be influencing your married life? Think about your own attitudes toward sexuality by checking the statements below:

_____ "It is important to me that we greet each other affectionately after being apart all day."

_____ "I like to be held and touched without always having intercourse."

_____ "I am easily embarrassed when I am nude."

_____ "Sex is too embarrassing for me to talk about."

_____ "I think that sex outside of marriage is okay."

_____ "I believe sex should be honored within the marriage covenant."

_____ "I think it's okay to use sex as a weapon or reward."

_____ "I think that the woman should do whatever the man wants."

_____ "I feel free to talk about my mate and our intimate sex life with my friends."

_____ "It is all right for the woman to initiate sexual activity."

_____ "I believe that a man should take the lead in sexual intercourse."

Do you see any patterns from your childhood reflected in your present life? More important, do you see conflict in your marriage now because your spouse doesn't like your way of doing something? Or were there such conflicts in the past that are now apparently resolved? Maybe they aren't. Burying them is not the same as resolving them.

In the deepest depths of every marriage lie the real reasons for behavior. Those reasons voice themselves if you listen carefully. What is your marriage trying to tell you?

Talk about these issues with your spouse. Then consider a sexual relationship covenant, like the one below:

_____ "I agree that we may differ on some things, and I agree to respect your opinion and feelings."

_____ "I agree to be open and honest about our sexual relationship."

_____ "I agree that the only way I can really please you is to let you guide me, and I am willing to do so."

_____ "I agree not to use sex as a weapon or reward."

_____ "I agree not to criticize or make fun of my mate's sexuality."

_____ "I believe that God's teaching and guidelines about sexual relationships are important and agree to make them a part of our marriage."

We've found that verbal or written covenants, such as this, form the foundation for an honest sexual relationship that undergirds any strong marriage.

Finally, after introspection and analysis, we always counsel couples to commit to lovemaking and romance in their marriage.

Commit to LoveMaking

Commit to lovemaking, not just as a recreational option available to married folks, but as a channel to deeper intimacy. It's one of the nicest things you and your spouse can do for each other.

But there is lovemaking and there is lovemaking.

Debi Newman points out, "There is fun sex versus meaningful sex. The world and media teach fun sex. It's exciting. In some cases the world even teaches to try different partners, which of course we certainly never would. Sex is uniquely designed for the marriage union. Outside marriage there's no commitment. That's not real intimacy. It's all physical, all on the surface. Outside the marital context, pleasure is its only goal.

"In contrast, meaningful sex is a special relationship with a particular person, an expression of emotional oneness as well as sexual release. Intimacy is the goal as well as pleasure. Sex and intimacy are not synonymous. Real intimacy is not truly available when you seek only pleasure. Intimate marital sex provides an emotional intensity greater than just the physical orgasm. Call it soul orgasm or emotional orgasm. Good marital sex gives physical pleasure secondarily."

Debi's advice becomes even more important as the marriage grows. Couples should be talking about sex throughout their marriage. Sexual intimacy is a journey. Partners who focus only on pleasure are bound to be disappointed eventually because there is only so much pleasure in the physical experience. Those who focus on intimacy find that the pleasures of sex never pale.

Commit to Romance

"But you just said that," you remind us. "'Commit to lovemaking.'"

No, we didn't, not exactly. Romance and sex are not synonymous. Romance deeply enhances sex, and sex vividly fulfills romance. Sex is lovemaking; romance is love-nurturing. Romance is holding hands, a heartfelt kiss that happened spontaneously, a rose on her pillow, a light in the window when he's coming home late. Romance is dinner for two. Most of all, romance is listening, truly listening, to the quiet of each other's heart.

As Frank Minirth puts it: "We have to move beyond our newlywed years in our marriage. But at the same time, we need to hold onto some of the feelings energized at this stage. We ought not lose all our idealism."

Mary Alice and Frank Minirth carve out time for each other. They date. They take walks and hold hands. This is romance. The old dream dreamt anew.

How do you hang onto the romance and the idealism in your relationship? Behavior helps. Do the same things you did when you dated. When you walk together, hold hands. Feelings drive our behavior, but behavior also drives our feelings.

"People get in trouble when they become disillusioned. When they see it's not perfect, they tend to bag it." Frank says.

Don't throw out idealism and romantic love, but hang onto it in the face of reality and imperfection. Work through the realism and other stages, but don't forget romantic love.

"Lose the romance? That would be a shame!"

It can be prevented by watching out for the . . .

Romance-killers

If romance is such a dandy thing, who in their right mind would ditch it? It gets scuttled by two major factors, time and conflict. As time goes by and the marriage matures, the fruits of misdirected maturation tend to quench romance. In our other books on later passages, we will look at this phenomenon.

But unresolved conflict—now there is a romance-killer you can do something about. Many sources of conflict arrive early and stay late in the union. Do some of these common sources of conflict sound familiar? Check the following to see if they apply to your marriage:

_____ Money—Who makes it, who spends it? Is it enough for the family needs?

_____ Control—Who makes the decisions in the family?

Does one spouse always try to take control of family decision making?

_____ Independence/Dependence—How much independence between the couple is too much, how much is too little? Does one spouse feel the other is too independent or conversely too dependent?

_____ Roles— Who does what jobs—mow the lawn, pay the bills, clean the house, cook the meals, run the errands, take care of the kids? Is one spouse always saddled with one job to his/her irritation?

_____ Parenting—Who raises the kids, who does the disciplining? Is the discipline of the kids a source of conflict between partners? Does only one spouse do the active parenting?

_____ Extended Family—Who has responsibility for taking care of the relatives? Is one marriage partner shouldering the responsibility of all extended family needs?

Conflict is normal, healthy, and can actually improve a marriage. Let's look at some of the ways to handle conflict properly and use it to your marriage's advantage.

Chapter 7

How Can Conflict Be Healthy?

"Conflict. It didn't take Frank and me long to find some," Mary Alice Minirth recalls. "Frank grew up in the country, where they eat heartily. His mom served at least three vegetables and two kinds of meat at every meal. I cooked the way my mother did: one vegetable, one kind of meat, potatoes or rice. And that was our conflict. Frank didn't need more food, he needed more choices.

"We got around it when we were able to recognize where it all came from: our families of origin. Together, we deliberately chose not to make this an issue."

Conflict is present in all relationships. Unfortunately, too many couples think "We mustn't have conflict, it'll hurt our marriage." But here's an equation we gave earlier:

1 person + 1 person = conflict.

It's corollary is also true:

1 person in love + 1 person in love = conflict anyway.

Conflict is inevitable, no matter what passage the couple is in. It is a normal part of any relationship. How the couple deal with conflict, however, can make or break a union.

Consider a medical doctor when presented with a particularly baffling case. The patient describes his symptoms and the doctor deduces from those symptoms what the course of action will be. Just like solving a mystery, the doctor must investigate the reason for the symptoms. He or she will order a whole battery of tests to help the investigation. Methodically, the doctor, perchance with the help of other physicians, will piece each test result together to come up with their best judgment of what is wrong with the patient. Only then will they begin to prescribe treatment they assume will have a positive effect.

Many times, though, the doctor has to settle for treating the symptoms. The actual ailment itself may or may not go away.

Analyzing conflict follows a similar pattern. We find in our practice that conflict is a symptom of a deeper issue.

Roots of Conflict

Married couples assume that conflict in their union causes separation. Actually conflict is not a cause; it is a symptom of something else. The wedge was already driven in between the couple and conflict was the result. Frequently when we counsel couples on conflict we hear the following:

"Where do you think your conflict comes from?" we ask.

The husband answers, "From her, she's always on my case."

To which the wife answers, "It's him. He does things that drive me right up the wall."

"What things?" we ask innocently.

"Tromping through the house with muddy shoes right after I've vacuumed. Working late and not even bothering to call. You know, inconsiderate things like that."

Where the real root to the conflict exists is somewhere else, somewhere deeper. We have learned that if you can find and deal with the deeper issue causing the wedge, the surface conflict can be successfully reached.

Frank Minirth explains, "We've found that unfinished business is a huge issue in marriage. People carry all kinds of conflict inside themselves because of their parents' issues and transfer them into their own marriage. As a result, conflict in their lives looks like it's coming from their marriage, but in reality it's coming from the past.

"Until the actual root of conflict is uncovered, there will be no resolution. It's like shooting at decoys. Decoys look like ducks. But you're never gonna hit a duck as long as you're shooting at decoys."

As we discussed before, hidden agendas, alias unfinished business from prior generations, is a big issue in a marriage and is a big root of conflict.

Behavior patterns you grew up with are far from the only source of conflict. Expectations your parents have for you and your spouse's parents have for him/her are also sources of conflict.

Remember the case of Rosie and Ralph. Ralph's father never fulfilled his success dreams in his career. As a result, he exerted subtle pressure on Ralph to achieve so that Ralph would care for him in his old age. Ralph reacted to that pressure by rebelling directly in the opposite way. He was so determined to not be a success and not be saddled with his elderly father that he still wasn't holding down a job at the age of twenty-six. He married Rosie so she could support him and he could continue his destructive rebellion against his father's expectations. This eventually created intense conflict between Rosie and Ralph.

Hidden agendas also rear their ugly head when they reside within either spouse and create conflict. Issues of which neither of you are aware may insidiously lie between the two of you, driving a wedge between your compatibility. We have found that premarital sexual experience, for example, can create such issues in a number of ways.

Consider this situation with Eliza and Bill Bradshaw. They didn't seriously consider marriage until they became sexually involved and Eliza insisted they wed. Bill did have several intimate girlfriends before, but it was time to settle down, he thought. He decided Eliza probably had a good point; it was the right thing to do. Trouble began not long after the wedding. He experienced sexual dysfunction and episodes of impotence. This had never happened to him before. Obviously, then, Eliza was to blame.

In intimate one-on-one counseling, Bill admitted, "I always did just fine before. What did Eliza do to me?"

"She made an honest man of you, and you can't stand it," would have been a bit too flip an answer and essentially incorrect. Rather, in conversation we helped Bill see how trapped he felt. In the past, his conscious mind told him, sexual activity had been a stolen delight. Now it was a duty. When you're married, you're required to perform. He felt coerced into marriage, coerced into a role of lover—like it or not. In further discussion, we identified other factors in his past as well. Once Bill dealt with these issues left over from his yesterdays—sorting true guilt from false guilt, asking and receiving forgiveness, and grieving through the issues—his love life blossomed.

Another source of conflict stems from the expectations you bring into the union.

I did it because . . .

"Why did you marry? Beyond love and attraction, what were the reasons down deep?" We ask that of each client. Some answers come up again and again.

Julia Karris said of her first marriage, "Why? Because Rick was such a catch! What I mean is, he looked like such a good catch. He was handsome, sophisticated, and he dressed well. He would talk to me in that sexy voice of his and I just melted."

And of her second husband, "Jerry. I married him because I thought he was the kind of person who could provide what I need, what I haven't gotten my whole life."

Louis Ajanian, the widower who remarried, "I married Marj, frankly, because I don't want to be alone in my old age. She's everything you could ever want in a woman, and I love her, but the loneliness; that's why."

Marj Ajanian, "I don't know. Getting married at my age is dumb, when you think about it. You wonder if it's worth it. Shucks. It takes ten years just to break him in."

Carl Warden, "I got married because that's what you did when you got out of school. Never occurred to me not to. I suppose it's not the best of reasons, but I suspect it's what sent a lot of the men from my generation to the altar."

How About You?

Why did you marry? Be honest, now, why, *really*? This is an important question, because your reasons for marrying, which seem so sensible and romantic at first, can become roots of conflict. Look over the following list and see if any of the reasons we've heard from our clients mirror yours. If not, add your reasons at the end:

_____ "I married him/her because everyone at my age was getting married. It was time."

_____ "I married because I wanted to have a family while I was still able to have children."

_____ "I married because I loved him/her."

_____ "I married my spouse because I wasn't getting any younger and I was afraid no one better would come along."

_____ "I married because that's what my parents expected me to do."

_____ "I married to get out of my parents' house and away from living under their roof and guidance."

_____ _____

_____

_____ _____

Now what about your spouse? Ask him/her to go through our list and privately write down his/her real reasons for marrying you. Then come together and discuss them. See how many unreal expectations you both brought into the marriage.

Unreal Expectations

One of the biggest movies, brand-new when Bess and Carl Warden married, was the Disney full-length feature cartoon, *Snow White and the Seven Dwarfs*—the quintessential good-triumphs-over-evil, happily-ever-after plot. Most of Disney's recent feature cartoons like *The Little Mermaid* and *Beauty and the Beast* also portray this good-over-evil and happily-ever-after plot. It is still as popular today as it was two generations ago.

Good-triumphs-over-evil summarizes propaganda supporting war efforts. And happily-ever-after summarizes marriage. Bess and Carl had every right to expect a perfect storybook marriage. So does every other couple today. It's promised them in a hundred unspoken ways. It's the "American way." It's an illusion.

In our practice, we never find a couple marrying to work on conflicts the new union might pose. They marry instead to get out of old problems, to escape dysfunctional families, and to perhaps erase the pain of a prior union gone sour. Or like Julia, to make up for all the losses and gaps of the past. Invariably, the old problems find their way into the new marriage, driving a wedge into the new partnership and becoming the taproot of conflict.

It is very important, even at this Second Passage, to dissect the deeper reasons for marrying. During the First Passage, the marriage is still young, fresh, and new. Conflict occurs, yes, but the excitement of the relationship can downplay the conflict. When idealistic love gives way to reality in this Second Passage of marriage, unresolved issues and conflict are more apparent as the real person and real relationship unfold. In counsel we also look for the very deep reasons people marry, the ones buried so far down that even they are not aware of them.

One such deep reason for getting married we have already mentioned: the couple marries with the idealistic notion that this new relationship will solve all relationship problems of the past. For Julia Karris, this was her conscious reason. In most people it is not. But it's still there.

Another recurring reason is to fix the wounded bird.

"What's a wounded bird?" Julia asked us during her counseling session.

"Two things, essentially," we replied. "For example, your parents are workaholics, is that correct?"

"That's understating it. Dad's also a neatness freak. For instance, he mows the lawn twice a week, not once, but twice—at least! The plush on my teddy bear was longer than the grass. He kept the barbecue spotless, the pool crystal clear . . . everything."

"Lots of love for you, but not time for affection."

"That's it exactly."

"One wounded bird, then, was your relationship with your parents. You hungered for attention; you rarely received it. In marriage you were going to get that attention. But that's not all. Deep inside, you were also going back to fix the original flawed relationship. Your heart was telling you, 'by succeeding with this man-woman relationship, I can change the past and correct how my parents were.'"

"That sounds crazy." Julia shook her head. "They weren't really that bad as parents, just busy and successful."

"They were splendid persons. But did you receive the nurturing and attention you needed?"

"They didn't mean to . . ." she protested, her eyes filling with tears.

"It's not a matter of fault. Did you or didn't you?"

"No." She crumpled her face in her hands. We handed her our ready box of tissues and continued when she was ready.

"That," we pointed out, "is all your heart knows. Your heart doesn't reason or make excuses. In fact, we've learned as we work with couples that a person frequently tends to marry someone like the parent he or she felt least loved by."

"You mean . . ." Julia frowned. "Rick is like my Dad in so many ways. So is Jerry. Not in looks so much, but in attitudes, actions. I never thought about it until now."

"If you feel your father loved you less than your mother did, you unconsciously marry someone like your father."

"I get it! By winning his love, I go back and undo the lack of love from the past. This time around it'll be different. Transfer, I transfer the love. Is that a good word for it?"

"That's a perfect word for it. Yes. This time around will be different."

And, so, into the marriage comes unreal expectations of the spouse. "I will make this relationship work to make up for the one with my parent(s) (or former spouse) that did not work." And, during this Second Passage, when these unreal expectations are popped like soap bubbles one by one, conflict results.

Another root of conflict comes from the real juice of a marriage: Who's in control.

The Juice

A retiring park ranger named Dwight and his wife were starting to look for a retirement home. They wanted peace and quiet, a rural atmosphere with no stress and pressure. They drove into the town of Beatty, Nevada, one day. Two dogs had just tangled in a snarling, flashing melee in the middle of the town's only cross street. Traffic casually drifted to a halt and waited as the dogs determined a winner. The larger dog fell to its back. The smaller cur stood over the loser a moment, then moved off. Traffic casually resumed.

"This is the place," Dwight announced.

They live in Beatty today, sipping lemonade on their porch as the rest of the world goes by. They even adopted one of the dogs.

Dwight and the dogs each illustrate a possible source of conflict that can put great stress on a marriage: the juice, power, control.

In the dogs, the picture is straightforward. They fought until one accepted loss by rolling on its back. That is where the term "top dog" comes from. Both dogs understood who was in control. End of conflict.

Dwight exercised immense power of a subtler sort. Where would this couple spend the rest of their lives? Dwight controlled that. If he were insensitive to his wife's desires, or if she adamantly opposed the lifestyle Beatty offered, the resulting power struggle could make the dogfight look tame. Or, his wife might let her resentment smolder, breeding anger and depression. She might, in numerous ways, try to usurp some of Dwight's control, or diminish it. None of this need be at the conscious level for it to spell disaster for the marriage.

Struggles for power and control are generally more noticeable in a new marriage where each spouse is testing the other's boundaries and control. In this Second Passage, power struggles can show up more profoundly as the couple polarizes from one extreme to the other in attempt to maintain a balance.

Polarization

We discussed polarization back in Chapter 3. Polarization is also an obvious source of conflict. When we enter into counseling with couples, we find that the statement "we never fight" is a big red flag indicating deep-seated troubles.

Carl Warden sat on his neighbor Bert's front porch. Bert boasted, "Meg and I have a perfect marriage. We never fight.

Meg is a proper wife, submissive. What I say goes." And he pounded his fist on the side of his rocker to emphasize the point.

Carl Warden pondered that for a few moments. "Not Bess. She always speaks her mind. I thank the Lord for her gumption or I would have found myself in a mess many times."

Bert's wife Meg simply gave in on every occasion. As time went by, it became easier and easier to do. And yet, Meg, fully as intelligent and capable of opinion as her husband, offered much of value to contribute. Angry at first that she had no effective voice, she resigned herself to the position frequently referred to as "doormat." The anger numbed out eventually, becoming depression. She lived a life free of conflict, but at a terrible price, and died a very miserable woman.

Bert and Meg were exhibiting this natural tendency of polarization that we warned you about in Chapter 3. As Bert became more and more dominant, Meg tended to become more and more submissive. Extreme polarization is very damaging.

Now think about our other case, Grace and Ron Chevington. Again, they polarized to an extreme degree. As Grace became more and more competent in her career and at home, Ron slid more and more downhill. His career at the television station began to suffer as he doubted his competence. He slacked off at home. And, even more alarming, he found solace in the bottom of a bottle. Alcohol provided an escape for him. If he was drinking he felt good. If he felt good, he felt competent. More than once, his producer had sent him home after smelling alcohol on his breath. He was on a downward spiral. Polarization in their marriage was destructive. Thank the Lord they didn't have kids yet.

Kids

The arrival of children in a marriage causes such profound changes many of which we discussed in Chapter 4. Suffice to say, even the most benign, lethargic child raises conflict factors between spouses exponentially.

When children come into a marriage from prior marriages, the conflict shoots even higher as we've already discussed. Jerry and Julia Karris found that out the hard way. Conflict was so prevalent in this family that they were hard pressed to tell us of a time when they weren't fighting.

So much was going wrong in this family. Where could we start? We talked to Greg, Julia's son from her former marriage. He seemed to be involved in most of the family conflicts. It took him three visits before he could truly open up. Although his natural father never took an interest in his son's life, Greg still held the fantasy that his real father would come around and be a more active parent. He not only fantasized it, he visualized it. Enter Jerry Karris. Suddenly there was a threat to this dream, no matter how unrealistic that dream might be. It took lots of talking to get Greg to see that his dad wasn't going to change for Greg's sake. Greg had to accept his dad for who he was. And, Greg had to begin giving Jerry Karris a chance.

On the other hand, Jerry Karris needed a lot of confidence boosting. He felt his worth as a parent was nil. So he stopped being one.

Greg was only one of Julia and Jerry's crises as a family. So much of their precious time and energy was spent just keeping their heads above water. Every time one issue seemed under control, sixteen more popped up. Their water-treading was failing—they were sinking. Their kids' needs were being neglected, their own needs were being neglected, and their marriage's needs were being neglected. We supported them as they reset priorities, strengthening their bond of intimacy while they helped Greg and the other children adjust to the union.

By the way, conflict also erupts between kids themselves, and parents find it extremely difficult to stay out of it. Since the purpose of this book is to deal with marriage, we will not give lengthy advice on parenting. We will, however, mention the fact we see proven over and over again: When a parent or another adult interferes with conflict between kids, the conflict moves from between the kids to between the child and parent or adult. The best rule is to stay out of their conflicts and let them solve them themselves. The exception, of course, is when the conflict threatens bodily harm. Then you must intervene to protect the safety of each child.

The best way for your children to learn to resolve their own conflicts is by observing how you and your spouse resolve your conflicts. Live the positive half of the adage: "Do as I do." Let your children see that conflict, acknowledgment, and resolution are parts of any normal relationship.

"Great!" you say. "I love a knock-down drag-em-out fight. So we'll just let 'er rip."

"That's not what we're saying at all," we protest. "Conflict is healthy if handled properly."

"How?" you ask.

Sticking to the Rules

In all the years of their marriage (forty-three in all), Bert and Meg never achieved anything close to intimacy. Bert would protest that he really loved Meg and we're sure he did. But he could not tell you how she felt about things and whether she had any hopes and dreams of her own. But Meg, like every other human being, craved deep intimacy and had dreams and aspirations for herself. Sadly, they were never realized.

Bess and Carl Warden's marriage, on the other hand, was full of intimacy. Friends and relatives constantly remarked how the two of them acted like newlyweds even after forty-eight years of marriage. When they had conflict, they "kept it honest." They both had a desire to avoid dirty fighting and to keep the conflict to the issue being debated. They did this by adhering to a few simple rules when resolving conflict in their relationship. Rules one and two address the deeper "cause" issues behind conflict, while rules three, four, and five give helpful tips on managing the "symptom" dimension of conflict.

1. Know Yourself.

First, you must understand what your position is and why you feel that way. You can begin to discern this by examining your own feelings. Why am I feeling this way? Why does this bother me so much? Are there any similarities between the way I am feeling now and how I felt growing up?

Obviously, in the heat of an argument it is very difficult to gain this objective point of view. This is why we suggest using a recent conflict with your spouse as a test case and apply the rules we're giving here to the conflict.

A simple exercise for you to do is to take a piece of paper and fold it in half lengthwise. Think of a recent conflict and on one side of the paper list the things you said in the argument, like:

"You're never home."

"What's more important to you, your job or our family?"

On the other side of the paper, list the corresponding thoughts you had for each statement, such as:

"I feel lonely, abandoned."

"I feel like I'm the only one taking care of this family."

Now think why you might have felt this way. Was there anything in your past that may have sneaked into your argument? Any time-release capsules?

One client of ours recognized a capsule in the heat of an argument with his wife over control of the checkbook. He suddenly sensed his old inadequacy fears kicking in. He was deeply, viscerally afraid of seeing himself as a loser and so had to have control of the purse strings in his family to prove his competence.

2. Think.

Television has rescued us from the need to analyze and think. A television episode goes through an unvarying pattern where the plot and problems are solved right on the screen before our very eyes. Some shows even go further, by analyzing and philosophizing in a recap during the last few minutes. Americans no longer feel any strong need to think. But, unless people are trained in the ability to look at alternatives and make decisions, they can never resolve conflicts.

You must think about what your spouse's position really is. Use debating skills you may have learned or seen in high school. In order to debate your own position effectively, you must thoroughly understand your opponent's position. Take a moment to think again about a recent conflict. List the areas where your mate's position has merit, for example:

"Her job is very stressful. Perhaps she feels a need to put in extra time."

Finally, try to weed out any time-release capsules that may be playing upon your spouse's or your feelings.

"My husband's father was a terrific success. I wonder if he feels that he also has to drive hard to be a success?"

3. Avoid Absolutes.

It's natural for arguing couples to throw missiles back and forth at each other. If both parties know themselves and are thinking, however, they can call a cease-fire to the accusations. This is much easier if you *never* speak in absolutes:

"You're *always* working late."

"You *never* come home to me and the kids."

"You *never* help around the house."

Absolute statements usually guarantee defensiveness because they're so overstated. A husband or wife may come home late one or two nights a week, but the other three or four nights he/she is at home. A husband may not pick up his laundry or vacuum, but he may do the dishes after dinner.

Instead of absolutes, try to speak specifically on the issue that is bothering you.

"I don't appreciate having to pick up your dirty clothes when the laundry basket is right there in the corner."

Another trap to avoid is character assassination or criticism. "You're so selfish, all you think about is yourself." How would you feel if someone said these things to you?

During their conflicts, Ron and Grace Chevington fell into this trap over and over. Grace could be downright cruel with her laconic remarks. Ron acted like her remarks rolled off him as water off a duck's back. But in reality, everything she said he took to heart and stored deep in his subconscious. Every time she criticized him and cut him down, he slid down one notch.

Their conflicts became deeply destructive. They weren't playing by the rules. It was ironic that Grace's hidden agenda was to marry Ron so her life would be devoid of conflict.

4. Stick to the Basics.

When Carl and Bess "kept it honest" as they fought, Carl meant essentially that they stayed with the basics. They kept to the issue being argued about.

"There is no way I'm going to pay $75 for tennis shoes for a teenager!" Jerry declared in the middle of the athletic shoe store at the mall one afternoon.

"But, Jerry, I think Kinsley deserves them. She's been very

helpful around the house. And, prestige is important to her. A lot of kids at her school wear these shoes," Julia said.

"That's easy for you to say. You're always coddling her. You don't do the bills. We can't afford to be careless like this. If you had your way, we'd spend our way into the poorhouse!" Jerry yelled.

"That's not true! I do what I can. I earn some of the money too. You never give me credit. You're way too hard on Kinsley and me," Julia lashed back.

Kinsley stood in the corner of the store, horrified at Julia and Jerry's yelling. Worse yet, she felt responsible for the argument. The Karrises had not kept the conflict to the issue being debated—whether or not to buy the pair of tennis shoes. They had let the conflict get personal.

If the argument is about dirty laundry on the floor, keep that as the main issue. If you are fighting about when a spouse is expected home at night, focus on that issue alone. Staying to one issue in an argument is easier said than done we know. So, how do you do it?

5. Keep Your Selves out of the Fight.

"But how do we do that? We're the ones fighting," you might protest.

Issues and persons are two different entities. Argue over the issues, but never allow your arguments to get personal. As much as you can, keep emotions out of it. When the need to win becomes so encompassing that it controls your emotions and thoughts, the disagreement then becomes a brutal dog-fight, invariably shredding love and egos. Dogs fight each other, they don't fight about issues. A constant equation here is:

Conflict − Rational Processes = Explosion.

You can avoid having the fight become personal and emotional by being creative and diffusing the situation.

Getting Creative

Debi Newman explains, "We frequently hear from our clients the statement, 'I never let a fight go overnight.' They'll do anything to resolve the conflict so they can go to sleep, even a quick fix. Or, they might deny their anger. Or else, they'll discuss it in bed, when they have their first free time together.

"We try to get the couple to see that a fight doesn't have to be resolved quickly or gotten rid of simply so they can go to sleep. By all means, we encourage them to address their anger before going to bed. One way of doing that may be to agree not to deal with the issue now, but set a definite time tomorrow to discuss it. You may not be able to sleep better, but it gives you cooling-off time."

Frank Minirth agrees, "Don't lie in bed, tired and frustrated, and expect to hash it out, whatever it is. You don't have the ability to look at options then. To be creative in dealing with conflict, you must be fresh enough to think."

Breathing space and cooling-off time are so crucial in a heated situation. It is not wasted time. Use it constructively. Work out physically, clean the garage, beat a rug, or clean the house. Do something physical to sap off the adrenaline that the anger ignited. Indeed, you may have to postpone your discussion more than once if your anger has not diffused. Write a letter to your spouse. Don't deliver it; burn it up when you're done. Just writing out your thoughts and feelings helps to clarify them.

Diffuse the Situation

Use anything you can think of to inject humor into the conflict. One couple we know takes their clothes off when in a heated argument. It's very difficult to argue in the nude!

Once understanding the rules of the game, the couple can proceed to resolution. But resolving the crisis and strengthening intimacy are not two separate processes. Three important things happen when a couple truly and completely resolve a conflict:

First, the conflict is completed. It won't rear its ugly head again in the union. Think how easily unresolved conflicts just keep resurfacing every time friction develops. That cycle of acrimony breaks when the conflict is dissolved.

Secondly, each person understands himself or herself better.

"Why did I get into this fight anyway? What are my deep-down motivations and attitudes? Should they be adjusted?" That introspection will serve the person well the next time conflict arises either inside or outside the marriage.

Thirdly, the couple know each other better. And that is the very heart of oneness. Done properly and well, crisis and conflict resolution encourages intimacy. Let's see how it works.

Conflict Resolution

Throughout all the passages of a marriage, the couple deal with conflict. Even though their attitudes will mature and change, the three ways to resolve conflict will always remain the same: (a) compromise, (b) agree to disagree, and (c) love gift.

Compromise

Everyone has given in a little in any relationship. Mary Alice Minirth did that with Frank's needs for dinner choices. "Now I give him more than one vegetable choice at night." But Frank has also given in a little on this issue, "I realized that I didn't need that many choices. Mary Alice didn't have to cook so many different entrees on my account."

Agree to Disagree

Debi Newman remembers such an issue in their marriage. "When I came home from work, the first thing I wanted to do was get out of my shoes. I kicked them off and laid back on the couch. I could finally wriggle my toes."

Brian Newman, "It drove me up the wall. She'd leave her shoes exactly where she kicked them off. Pretty soon, there were several pairs of shoes all over the living room. I decided to teach her a lesson. So I'd pick up her shoes and put them away in a different box or place."

Debi Newman smiles. "I can laugh about it now, but I hated not knowing where my shoes were in the morning. I felt Brian was infringing upon my rights. We still don't agree on this issue. I don't feel I have to pick up my shoes right after I take them off. He does."

Brian adds, "Now, when Debi kicks off her shoes, instead of hiding them in a secret place, I put her shoes neatly in a corner of the living room out of the way."

Love Gift

Carl Warden remembers one situation, "When I was a young buck, a long time ago, I really wanted one of those new motorcycles, an Indian. Remember the Indians? Bess wouldn't hear of it. We didn't have all that much money and Bess wanted a more reliable automobile, not a motorcycle. 'What if we have a baby? How could we take it on a motorcycle?' she protested. She was also afraid for my safety. She was right of course, my desire wasn't too practical. I just wanted one. On the other hand, we already had an automobile. But I gave in to her on this one."

A love gift is exactly that: giving in. A love gift says, "For whatever reasons, I'm giving in on this issue. I may feel as strongly as you do, but I'm willing to give you your choice." It has to be done without anger or resentment or it isn't a healthy response.

Carl's friends, Bert and Meg illustrate this. Meg gave in every time. That's where a love gift became, with time, a cop-out, neither love nor a gift.

None of these three methods of resolution is appropriate to every situation. Sometimes, for example, compromise is the best; other times it's not possible. Be aware, though, of becoming locked into one approach at the exclusion of the other two as Bert and Meg did.

Resolution

Although you cannot always expect perfect resolution, you must always look toward eventual resolution. The alternatives are easily seen in the following equations:

Conflict − Resolution = Alienation

Conflict + Resolution = Intimacy

The argument left unsettled, the anger not dealt with, the opinions unvoiced, keeps the conflict unresolved. All these "un's" become a wedge driven between the couple. If a couple separates, we find that the separation begins long before it surfaces. Anger and resentment must be dealt with, and forgiveness must be given.

Chapter 8

The Ultimate Adjustment

T he kids were crabby. They were always crabby around suppertime. The six-year-old was whining about nothing to do, the four-year-old was being the clinging, sniveling little brat she usually was, and the baby was howling. 5:16 P.M.

With the baby in the backpack and the four-year-old wrapped around her thigh, Meg Frost cut up some carrots into the one-pot dinner and clapped the lid on. She hacked up a tomato for the salads. The six-year-old came wandering into the kitchen for the hundredth time, saw the tomato and groused bitterly about how he hated tomatoes and why did he have to eat them? 5:20.

She glanced out the window. There was the broken garage window, still not fixed. And the grass was getting tall enough to hide beachballs in. Don promised three days ago he was going to mow it. So much for promises. 5:21.

The air conditioner started thumping. She peeled the four-year-old off her leg and ran to throw the switch before it burned the pump motor out again. Don said it was all right! He told her, "Sure, sure, it won't go out again" in that maddeningly patronizing voice of his. She hated that tone he too often took, mollifying the little woman with a few hollow words. Now she had the privilege of sitting in Dallas in the

summer heat for another four days and listening to the kids
while the air conditioner man got around to visiting. 5:23.

Peachy. Sex was going to go downhill, just watch. When it
was hot and stuffy in the house, neither she nor Don would feel
much like it, and sex hadn't been all that great the last few
months to start with. Why was summer always blah time?

She lifted the lid on the stew pot to stir the carrots
throughly.

Here came Don breezing in the back door like a lark on
happiness pills. He shot a cheery, "Hi, Hon. Sorry I'm late"
her way.

She threw the pot lid at him.

Dealing with It All

. . . All at once. The various issues affecting the Second
Passage of marriage do not happen in discrete little bundles, to
be dealt with one at a time before the fireplace on a quiet
winter evening with a cup of tea in your hand. They must be
dealt with all in a jumble during the heat of battle. Meg Frost
was being pressed by the heat of battle (not to mention the
defunct air conditioner)—the kids, the problems, the unmet
promises, and yes, some sexual baggage.

Put them all together, they spell A N G E R. And they invariably come all together, each issue clamoring at once for her full
attention just the way her three kids did.

To strengthen and solidify her marriage, Meg was going to
have to deal with each of the issues we discussed to this point.
That takes time. And to bring some peace to her life while she
did all that, she was going to have to somehow come to terms
with her anger and frustration.

Anger

Most medical practitioners agree that in our modern society,
up to 50 percent of physical disorders are significantly stress-
related. Anger, resentment, and fear are powerful stressors (We
recommend the book *Worry-Free Living* by Dr. Frank Minirth,
Dr. Paul Meier, and Don Hawkins for a more detailed discussion of the effects of anger and other stressors.). Meg faces

more than just some resentment and unhappiness. She could damage herself physically as her fury simmers untreated.

How Anger Operates

Ask Meg what makes her angry and she would tell you about the promises Don failed to keep, about the little things constantly going wrong. She would say the kids anger her (actually, what they do is irritate; that's not the same thing, exactly). What she would not realize is that those were simply the targets, the things the head dwells upon. It's in the heart that anger begins, and it is born not of lost promises but of fear.

"Ridiculous!" Meg would snort. "What am I afraid of?" And on the surface it sounds ridiculous. But down deep, in the recesses of her heart where Meg Frost doesn't bother to explore, she is desperately afraid of being hurt. She fears that Don will renege on other promises, promises more important than a mere pledge to mow the lawn. She fears that Don will fall short when she needs him most. Indeed, she needs him right now and he's not here. He's late.

She fears she won't be a good mother to her kids. She doesn't admit it to herself, but her irritations at her kids worry her. Is she going to hurt them or damage them somehow if that irritation and impatience get out of hand?

All people harbor fears. Some have far greater fears than others. Fears are frightening. So the heart converts them into anger, but the head says you must be angry with something or about something. So the head picks a target. Often that target is a piece of evidence that fuels the fear.

Meg picked a target too. Fortunately, the pot lid missed.

Understand, not every single anger is born of fear. Things can happen to you from outside your sphere of influence. A mugger knocks you down and snatches your purse. The boss at work undercuts you and gives someone else the raise or promotion that should have been yours. Your anger is generated by an outside source, that hoodlum. But most anger, keep in mind, has a fear source.

How Anger Ends Up

Here's another formula we've learned:

unresolved anger = bitterness.

Anger into bitterness. Logical, when you think about it. And when you think about the extension, you realize that bitterness smothers intimacy. It was happening in Meg and Don's case—in Meg especially.

Don, too, was affected. Don realized his bride was not perfect after all. He got annoyed with the kids too. And at a far deeper level he feared. Would he be an adequate father? Could he provide for this noisy, churning, growing, demanding family?

Could he hold onto his wife? The worst, the very worst, possible nightmare for a man is that some other man will steal the affections of his wife and children. That fear persists, deep inside.

And so, anger and resentment and bitterness quench intimacy. They destroy not just sexual intimacy but the full range of closeness married persons ought to be enjoying. If you fear being hurt by a person, you understandably will not feel comfortable being close to that person, much less deliberately make yourself vulnerable. And increased intimacy is increased vulnerability.

Dealing With The Anger

Meg Frost would be the first to tell you that her anger cannot be dealt with. When one thing she's angry about gets resolved, something else pops up. You can't win. But that's not so.

New targets for anger do not mean new sources of anger necessarily. It might be the same deep fear, with the head picking a new target. Still, dealing with the target is important. The anger born of fear has become an entity in itself and must be handled as an entity, in addition to the fear. Meg has several options. Sometimes she can remove the target. Sometimes she can find the root fear and dig it out. And in any case she can forgive.

However she handles the surface anger, she is on the right road to resolving all the issues of this Second Passage. For surface anger blinds the marriage partners. They fix their attention on the anger and never get to the real issues. As Frank Minirth phrases it, "It's like going duck hunting. Decoys look just like real ducks. But if you shoot at the decoys, you're never going to get a duck."

Fear

Finding the Fear

How can Meg Frost identify those fears so deep inside her heart? So often, they arise from the very issues we've been talking about—sexual baggage, kids, conflicts, hidden agendas, the ugly head of reality rearing itself.

A friend of ours—let's call her Cheryl—complained, "When I'm sick my husband tries to belittle my illness. He'll say, 'Oh, come on. That's nothing.' He even gets mad at me for being ill! What kind of support is that? It infuriates me!" Her husband (we'll call him Ted) agreed with her all the way. "I suppose if something physical happened to her; some traumatic accident or something you could see; I wouldn't do that. But sick people, you know, they look the same as when they're well. You have a headache or bite your tongue, nobody knows it but you."

That, we reminded him, did not address the issue. Ted had to think a long time about Cheryl's accusation and the reasons he might actually be the way she accused. He thought about his childhood, things his parents and others told him, and other possible sources of misinformation or hidden agendas.

And he apparently hit upon it. He told us, "My mom got sick a lot while I was growing up. She couldn't take care of us kids and never was involved in any of our activities because of her physical condition. I really got tired of Mom's constantly recurring illnesses. I came to resent it, and I got really angry."

Ding! Time-capsule.

"What underlying fear could that generate?" we asked.

And he came up with that in no time at all. "I can think of two. One is, I'm deep-down afraid Cheryl will turn out like my mom. Actually, Cheryl isn't sick as much as most people. She's really very healthy. But that fear is there, right?"

"Right."

"And then there's the fear of being neglected—of Cheryl neglecting me because she's sick, like Mom did." Here was a holdover from his youth, unresolved anger he had to work through, a source of deep-seated fear.

Ted could work on the fear by self-talk, telling himself the same things about Cheryl's good health he told us. He could also remind himself that this was indeed an echo from the past not based on the reality of the present. Knowing about time capsules is a splendid help in defusing them.

And, Ted needed to ask Cheryl's forgiveness. He had to forgive his mom, too, whether she was still alive or not (it happens, she was), and thereby resolve the anger.

Other Layers

As you probe around, you may discover a separate layer between the anger and the fear. Disappointment or disillusionment, usually based on fears, can themselves generate anger. These, too, can profoundly influence your stress level.

A simple example is in-laws.

Ask Meg about her in-laws and she'll tell you about a sweet old couple who would like nothing better than to drive over her with a road grader. They seemed so nice at first, and they turned out to be wolves in sheep's clothing.

We asked Meg about her childhood. "Have problems with your parents?"

"Funny you should ask. Mom was a perfectionist. I could never do anything right. And Dad was a workaholic. I never saw him. But," she hastened to add, "I've worked through all that. It's okay now."

"You're aware of the dream-quest for perfect parents."

"Where every kid thinks his parents are perfect, and then he finds out they're not, and then he wishes they were. Yeah."

"Nearly every married person still seeks that perfect parent. And there is a deep underlying feeling that even though that person's own parents fell short, perfect parents are out there somewhere."

"Whoa!" Meg scrunched her face up. "You mean, I was assuming down inside that I was marrying into perfect parents?"

"You, and Don, and just about everyone else."

"That's weird!"

Most of what goes on sub-surface is weird. Meg hoped that her in-laws would be all the things her own parents were not. When the kindly old couple fell short, Meg projected her disappointment onto them. The disappointment actually arose within herself. They were the target, the visible source.

Further, anyone not dealing with family-of-origin issues (that is, unfinished business, lack of nurturing and such) is going to have in-law trouble. And that will generate anger.

It works the other way too. In-laws who didn't resolve their own issues often transfer them onto the kids.

How do you know it's happening? If you suffer chronic, constant anger, resentment, and tension with your in-laws, rest assured projection is involved. That's how to recognize it.

As you work on the hidden agendas of Chapter 5, you will uncover other sources of anger, with underlying sources of fear, disappointment, and frustration. Good! Obviously, that's all to your benefit, yours and your spouse's.

Ferreting Out Fear

In your own life, a lot of daily bumps generate irritation. Your mate does something and anger burgeons. Stop for a moment and think about the anger in your life, and secondly about its possible sources.

In the last day or two my anger has been kindled against these targets (be specific; Meg with the garage window, Ted with Cheryl's illness e.g.; not just "Don" or "Cheryl"):

1. _____
2. _____
3. _____

I understand these are the surface sources of my anger, but they may well reflect the inner sources.

Re: target #1 listed above:

This has _____ has not _____ come up in the past.

A similar target has come up in the past (the unmown lawn and broken garage window would be similar; both are failed promises):

_____

_____

After exploring my past and my memories, I think a possible fear that might underlie that target is:

_____

_____

_____

_____

Do this same exercise for any other targets, surface reasons for anger that you identified. What are the common threads? Is there more than one fear at work here, or are they all manifestations of one biggie? Do you see any intermediate layers?

Resolution

Anger always begets anger. Don wasn't at all happy about that pot lid whizzing at him. Meg wasn't at all happy about his failure to carry through with jobs around the house. He was mad at her for thinking he could wangle a 26-hour day in order to get everything done that she thought needed doing. They fumed at each other right up to bedtime and beyond.

It takes time to identify underlying fears. Days. Longer. And no person in the heat of anger is going to sit down and start exploring the possibility of deep, dark fears below conscious level. Anger does not permit that sort of cool introspection.

Anger must be handled on site, preferably right away.

"A lot of issues that generate anger—that are the targets," says Dr. Brian Newman, "cannot be handled instantly. You need a cooling-off period. It's perfectly okay to say, 'I'm furious. I have to back off and let it cool awhile before we talk about it, or we'll both just get angrier.' But if you say that, you should also make a definite appointment. Right. A genuine appointment, with a time and place, to sit down and talk it through. The anger issue is not resolved instantly because it cannot be. Not safely. But it will be. And that in itself is a great little cooler-offer."

First Step: Identify the Target:

You just did that.

Second Step: Make a Note to Identify Deeper Sources

Mark a time on your calendar when you can pause to think about the episode of intense anger that just occurred, or is occurring.

That sounds dumb.

Dumb like a fox. And do you know? You should write down exactly the target of your anger because a day from now you may not be able to remember just what it was. Anger's like that. The head doesn't really care about the target. It's a ploy, remember, for sidetracking fear. So jot it down. You'll work on it later.

Third Step: Work on Forgiveness

Forgiveness is such a misunderstood concept. The person doing the forgiving—the forgiver—assumes he or she is doing the recipient (the forgivee) a favor, letting the recipient off the hook. Then the forgiver assumes that what has been forgiven must be forgotten. Neither assumption is so.

The person who receives the most from an act of forgiveness is the person doing the forgiving. It is for that person, more so than for the recipient, that God ordained forgiveness.

And forgiving does not mean forgetting. Forgiving is the only good healthy way to process the anger that comes from both inner fears and the transgressions of others.

Picture a situation you've seen in the newspaper from time to time. Fiend X murders an innocent child. The father of the child, F, says, "I forgive X for killing my baby." The world says, "How can he do that? How can he condone X's fiendishness?" F isn't condoning it at all. He certainly can never forget it. F is taking the final step in resolving his own fury through the act of forgiveness.

Forgiveness is tough. Does Meg have to? Do you? Yep. It is expected of you. By whom? By God. When Peter asked how many times one ought to forgive, Jesus answered, seventy-times seven, meaning in the vernacular of that day not so much four-hundred and ninety times as an endless number of times. Even taken literally, we're talking daily forgiveness here. That whole passage, Matthew 18:21–35, is most instructive regarding God's attitude toward forgiveness.

Every married couple must, therefore, master the ability to forgive, especially since forgiveness is an essential part of the grieving process. It's a skill that must be practiced daily, for man and wife are constantly exposed to little hurts and major problems.

Don't forget, while you're at it, to forgive yourself when necessary. You let yourself down. You're less than the complete and perfect person you want to be. You get angry with yourself for flubbing. Forgiving oneself is just as important as forgiving others.

The Mechanics of Forgiveness

1. Admit Your Feelings

Identify the hurt and pain in life. These are the targets, the surface sources of anger. Whether they arose from an inner fear or were imposed from the outside, they need to be dealt with.

2. Commit to Forgive

It's easy to say you'll work on forgiving. It's not so easy to commit yourself to what may be a long, long haul. Meg will still be looking at that broken garage window a week from now because Don isn't going to get around to fixing it. He'll mow the lawn, but it will grow again. The kids won't quit whining just because Meg forgives them for doing it.

Forgiveness doesn't erase the past or the effects of the past.

3. Give a Little

Give what? Yield up your right to retribution. You must voluntarily turn over to God your rights of retaliation, however major or minor. "Vengeance is mine," saith the Lord (Heb. 10:30). In part, that's because He's so much better at it than you could ever hope to be.

We are not talking here about legal actions and contexts. The crime victim is called upon to forgive the criminal, but certainly not, by withdrawing testimony or charges, to stymie justice.

Remember that you are forgiving the person, not the act. Therefore the statement "Forgiving means putting my stamp

of approval on an unforgivable act. I cannot condone the act"
is without merit. Do you see the difference between the sin and
the sinner? That is the difference you must make as you forgive
and forgive again.

4. Work on Restoring the Relationship

Meg can forgive Don for failing to come through for her in
the ways she thought he should, but there is still the matter of
warming up to him, in bed and in other intimacies. Thanks to
the air conditioner, that's literal as well as figurative.

Don can forgive her for that pot lid, but down inside he will
long harbor the distrust the incident fostered. When will be the
next time he walks in the door and something blows up in his
face?

Forgiveness doesn't really erase the past, leaving the past to
continue to haunt you. Don got off easy with the pot lid. We
have found that in marriages where a major source of distrust
occurred—an episode of infidelity, for example—six months to
two years elapse before the couple can get back up to the level
of intimacy they previously enjoyed.

In the exercise a few pages back, you identified some episodes of anger. For each one of them, work these questions
through:

What specifically was I angry at or about? _____

_____

Whom specifically should I forgive for this episode? _____

_____

I am _____ am not _____ ready to keep that forgiveness
functional in the long term, even when the same targets happen
again.

I am _____ am not _____ ready to give up any chance to
retaliate.

I am _____ am not _____ ready to restore our relationship. I recognize that even if my spouse was not the target of
my anger, or at fault, my anger affects our marital relationship.

I will make this specific move toward improving our relationship in the wake of the episode of anger (a treat for the spouse,

making love, a few words of apology or affection, nothing at all . . .) _____

_____

_____

But what about all the other issues we've discussed? Let's look at it like a forest firefighter does.

The Time to Work Out Kinks

A tool of forest management today's forest rangers use is the controlled burn. It's a fire deliberately set in a forest so as to burn off ground cover and duff—leaves and sticks—before it gets too deep. Deep duff when burnt can kill the trees and understory. Shallow duff burns off safely.

To conduct a controlled burn, the firefighters do whatever they must to contain their fire in a certain area. Then they walk around with a drip torch, a device that literally drops tiny little fires as it goes. They burn off small portions of duff at a time until the job is done. Now, should lightning or carelessness ignite a fire, it won't kill the trees. Most of its fuel has been safely removed.

Meg was consumed not by a raging fire but by a whole lot of tiny little fires. Those fires were constantly being ignited by this and that. She'd try to stomp out one and two more would flare up. She never was going to get around to working on all these other issues when she was in a constant state of anger and irritation.

True forgiveness—the management of anger—puts out the fires long enough that Meg can explore the other issues of her marriage.

We do not mean to imply that managing anger through for-giveness is a stopgap measure until you can get to the real issues —finding out your inner fears, handling your sexual baggage, the hidden agendas, all that. Anger and forgiveness are issues in themselves.

And they ease the friction. They improve the atmosphere. Moreover, they make you feel more like working on those knotty issues.

Make yourself a list. With a space of several lines between each, write down:

1. _____ Imperfections in My Mate
2. _____ Sexual Baggage
3. _____ The Kids, Bless Them
4. _____ Conflicts
5. _____ Hidden Agendas
6. _____ Hidden Fears I've Found
7. _____ Things Generating Anger That Happened to Me

Make another list now, on the back side of the same piece of paper if possible:
Things I learned about it
(and halfway down the page)
Things I'm going to do about it with my spouse
These are your job specifications. Every job position in industry has its job specs, the things you have to do in that job. These are marriage job specs. As you work on each of the seven items, thinking about them, exploring your own and your spouse's attitudes and past, jot yourself notes. On the back side, under, for example, "Things I learned," you need only write the number of the topic and a few words of reminder.
"#6—Mom feared abandonment. So do I."
"#1—She'll never get her act together re: housekeeping/not organized."
And so on.
This will help you stay on the track when exploring the deeper issues of your union.

A New Reason to Be Married

If the anger and resentment are resolved, and the issues worked on, how do we restore this relationship? Meg and Don, and Tom and Marsha had to write new contracts. So do you. Let's consider that next.

Chapter 9

Can You Write a New Marriage Contract?

*J*oe Jacobs stared glumly at his bridge hand. He had an ace and three low-number cards. Barbara had just bid two spades. Now what was he supposed to do? He was supposed to do something when this situation came up. He couldn't remember.

"What am I doing here?" he burst out.

Barbara frowned at him. "You're supposed to be learning how to play bridge, that's what. But you're not trying. You're not concentrating. Don't you want to be a good bridge player?"

Her question cleared Joe's mind. Suddenly he realized what was going on, and what he was going to do about it. "No, Barbara, I don't want to be a good bridge player. I don't want to be a bad bridge player. I don't want to be any kind of bridge player. I don't like the game." He dropped his cards facedown on the table. "You learn bridge. I'm going down to the armory. I'll pick you up afterward." And he left the community building, left Barbara with her bridge lessons and her constant parade of activities.

Driving over to the armory, he tried to sort things out. Barbara knew his AA meetings were Tuesday and Friday. Yet she had scheduled these Tuesday night bridge lessons deliberately; he could see that now; a ploy to draw him away from AA. She

154

was always finding something to do on Fridays too. Or she'd say, "You look too tired tonight. Why don't you just stay home?"

Why was she trying to keep him away from AA? It was she who intervened to get him there in the first place. She was the one who confronted him about his drinking, who fought him just as stubbornly when he resisted stubbornly, who helped him return to a cautious sobriety. She was responsible for his recovery. Why was she trying so hard to sabotage it now?

Joe walked into the AA meeting more than an hour late, but they greeted him heartily anyway. He settled into a folding chair with a happy smile, home at last. "Gentlemen," he announced, "I have just played my last bridge game."

Joe and Barbara's marriage presents an intriguing picture of how powerfully the hidden forces of a secret marriage contract work. Joe puzzled over the surface indications, such as Barbara's peculiar resistance to recovery. AA helped him see what was happening below the surface—that Barbara, accustomed to being in control and handling everything, was suddenly finding herself with reduced responsibility, as Joe took over his own life. Barbara was losing power, and that frightened her, particularly because she could not yet trust Joe's competence. But in the third layer, hidden contracts based on hidden agendas exerted their ultimate influence.

Barbara's father had been an alcoholic. It follows that she would marry one; children of alcoholics so often do. In fact, her mother had, for Grandpa Bill "liked his booze." Barbara determined that she would achieve what her mother and grandmother never could: straighten out her man. With the help of Dr. Robert Hemfelt and the clinic, she arranged an intervention in which Joe was confronted by the severity of his drinking problem. As part of the recovery, Brian Newman counseled Barbara and Joe regarding marital health, and Robert treated Joe's alcoholism in group therapy. It worked. For six months now, Joe had kept his sobriety.

Trouble began, though, from the day Joe began to recover. Barbara repeatedly phoned Brian, giving advice, telling him what to do in the counseling sessions. In essence, she was trying to exert control, to shape Joe in the mold of her choosing, to be a co-therapist because she knew Joe best. When Brian confronted her with her unseen agenda, she canceled therapy and tried to talk Joe out of going. Barbara accused Joe and Brian of causing unnecessary conflict. She claimed therapy was making things worse. But poor Joe could see he was becoming better, feeling stronger, getting back in touch with sexuality, growing spiritually. What was this message from Barbara that their marriage was getting worse?

The below-the-surface forces are familiar to anyone who knows about codependency. As long as Joe was drinking, Barbara controlled everything. When Joe came back to life, requesting and enjoying sex more, expecting a say-so in finances, resuming an active role as husband, Barbara had to share control. It was healthy for Joe to share responsibility, but it was threatening for her.

Deeper, darker, forces worked here, however. Barbara struggled with two hidden contracts working at cross purposes. First, try as she might, Mom never did succeed in fixing Dad, so Barbara had to try to fix her husband. At the same time, a second agenda competed with the first: A woman's single most important, significant, and noble role is to hang in there in the face of adversity. Take care of the dysfunctional spouse.

It would seem Barbara couldn't have them both. So long as Joe was sick, though, the contracts were compatible with the operative word in the first agenda: *try* to fix. Also, they fit in with Barbara's past; this was how she grew up.

Ah, but once Joe made his U-turn, the first contract negated past history and the second contract couldn't exist at all. Barbara no longer had to take care of a dysfunctional spouse. Down deep, where her conscious thoughts never ventured, Barbara felt disloyal to Mom because the only role Mom ever modeled was of the stoic, the long-sufferer. The bottom line was: Without a sick Joe to take care of, neither Barbara nor her marriage had any purpose. And that, unconscious though it was, frightened her to distraction.

Barbara's contracts, which were so interwoven with Joe's alcoholism, had been voided. She needed to get a new one if her marriage and her life were to have purpose. The fourth task of this Second Passage of marriage is to write a new marriage contract.

The Fourth Task: Write a New Marriage Contract

In order to build a relevant contract, the couple must identify the sore spots they will have to attend.

Even in the healthiest marriage there come times, usually during the shift from one passage to the next, when a new contract becomes necessary. As unions mature, we all need new reasons to remain married. Also, the times themselves change, altering spouses' roles in society and in the home. Taken step by step, writing a new contract is not difficult, but it should be painstaking. As Christians, we have a steadfast commitment to honor lifelong marriage. One of the finest ways to honor that commitment is to rediscover and reaffirm new ways of being together as we mature from passage to passage.

It should be noted, that even if a couple didn't prepare a contract as part of the early years of their marriage, it's not too late to write one now. By an existing contract, we mean several things: a contract you wrote as part of Passage One or hidden contracts working in your subconscious. Let's examine those latter contracts.

First Review the Existing Contracts

You already laid important groundwork when you inventoried your parents' and grandparents' marital contracts and agendas in Chapter 5. We now see how the past wields its weight. The phenomenon involved is called "splitting off."

In psychology jargon, you address each aspect of yourself by either owning it—accepting it and dealing with it—or splitting it off. Picture a family as magnets lying on a table, the big magnets being the parents, the little ones the kids. On the table we dump a spoonful of iron filings labeled, let's say, sexuality. Normally, everyone has some. But the two big magnets for some reason refuse to own their sexuality (sexuality is a common factor in owning and splitting off). They reverse their polarity. Split off from where they ought to go, the filings leap like wild cards elsewhere onto other magnets where they do not belong.

Normally, if a major area of feeling or personality is split off, it goes into the next generation's marriage as hidden agendas. That marriage will either mimic or amplify it, cure or compensate, or rebel against it . . . and eventually, pass it on.

Remember the case of Ian and Rhoda, where Rhoda was extremely promiscuous prior to marriage and then shut down sexually after she married Ian? Her problems were tied to past generational issues. In Rhoda's case, her grandmother's sexual excess generated shame in her mother. Promiscuity and shame came together in Rhoda's "I will have a sexless marriage." It did not surprise us to learn that Rhoda's two brothers both suffered sexual dysfunctions that neither ever discussed. All the children of the parents' union will feel the effect in some way, whether there be one child or a dozen.

Good news! We have learned that families communicate across the generations in remarkable ways, transcending time and place. If Grandma and/or Mom change, the daughter benefits. A full cure does not come down from above that way, for the daughter still has a lifetime of unspoken messages to deal with and she must take responsibility for her own marriage. But any improvement in the parents' lives, however belated, will help her. Neither is geography a barrier. If something major shifts in the family dynamics, even if the parents live in New Jersey and the children are scattered through four western states, the shift will be felt.

As a first step to writing a new contract, then, you will want to identify all the old ones—yours and those of the past, stated and unstated. Normally we ask each marital partner to work independently at this, then compare notes.

So let's begin. You've already done most of the groundwork for this by identifying those hidden agendas, ferreting out any sexual baggage you carry, resolving conflict, and ameliorating your anger by forgiving.

Drafting the New Contract

These problem items become the basis for establishing new contract items, in part. Your new contract will adjust or reverse the dysfunctional items. It will also cover items beyond the hidden agendas. It should prevent future problems, if possible, as well as solve past difficulties. We're now ready to write exciting new reasons to be married.

"I'm afraid," Ian admitted. "We ran into problems because my hidden contract said sex is all right outside marriage. Now I'm replacing it with 'Sex must stay inside the marriage.' I don't think I can carry it out. Especially if Rhoda can't come around too—you know."

"Do you think," we asked, "that every person who commits adultery has a hidden contract telling him or her it's all right?"

Ian shrugged. "Got me. Do they?"

"No. Hidden contracts do not control a 100 percent of anyone's actions. A person with a healthy unspoken contract may well fall to temptation, especially if the tempter's contract is a powerful one. And the reverse is true. You can easily fall to temptation, and you must guard against that carefully. But you're no different from everyone else. We all are tempted by wrong, regardless of the contract—sex, dishonesty, every kind of wrong."

"I see." Ian smiled. "The contract just makes it lots, lots easier."

Exactly.

Our clients first sketched the broad parameters of their contract. The basics. We suggest you do so also.

A Statement of Commitment

Determined to be honest, Barbara, the alcoholic's wife, wrote down, "I am committed. I thought about leaving, but I will not consider that again for at least a year."

You must be honest also.

It is valuable to *state some affirmation about each other and the marriage.* Joe wrote, "Barbara brought me back from the dead, literally, and I won't abandon her. I'll put her and our marriage first."

Make certain in all this that you've established the underlying agenda upon which you will base your new contract.

Take a moment now to write your statement of commitment.

Before you write your new contract, let's look at some common dysfunctional contracts we've seen in couples, so you can avoid them.

Major Mutual Contract Issues

Consider these common contracts in two ways: (1) Do any sound like something that could be controlling your marital behavior? (2) Just for practice, how would you write a new contract to counteract each of these, laying the foundation for a healthier union? Notice how detailed you can get.

- "My spouse is an emotional punching bag through which I release anger toward other people (or, sometimes, even expunge my parents' anger toward others)."
- "I picked my spouse just to prove my parents were right—or wrong—about the opposite sex, another race, a different class."
- "I picked a wounded bird to rescue because he/she needs me and won't fly away; in that way I can fix what went wrong a generation ago, and besides, with all the emotional hassle, I won't have to become vulnerable with true intimacy."
- "My spouse is an extreme opposite of one of my parents, so I will not have to suffer the way I did when I lived with that parent."
- "I need to be punished because I have lots of family-based shame to be paid for, so I picked an abusive spouse."

Those are perhaps the most common; the list goes on. List two of the old contracts in your own marriage:

1. _____

_____

2. _____

_____

Do these two require change? If so, in what way? Write a new contract entry for each of those old agendas:

1. _____

2. _____

Now down to the nitty-gritty. Having sketched the broad strokes of a solid contract, get specific about the details. Your new agreement and your revised agenda should both repeat what is best about your existing contract and also be the antithesis of whatever was dysfunctional about the old one. Here are some prompts to help you.

Spiritual Matters

There is a difference of opinion in the Christian church between the liberals and conservatives. Unfortunately, that opinion extended right to Louie Ajanian's hearth. His wife, Marj, was conservative, he liberal. She would argue for as long as it took to get him to accept an inerrant Scripture. He refused to argue. She wanted to keep the faith simple. He liked lots of liturgy and vestments and furbelows. She claimed she would have nailed Ninety-five Theses to his bedroom door, had she been able to find the hammer.

As they plowed through their Second Passage of marriage, Lou and Marj had to establish two sets of balances. When feelings and faith wax hot, spouses like the Ajanians may find themselves in a battle to pull each other into a certain interpretation. That was happening to Lou and Marj, as much as Lou would allow. Therefore, they first had to find common ground. This common foundation permits a common spiritual bond that can stand against the differences. Along with union, the Ajanians must have autonomy in their faith. They must each find God, as individuals, and as a couple. They sought balance between divergent views, based on that common ground, and balance between serving God as an individual and as a team.

This was no small thing for the Ajanians, who shared much common ground in their religious beliefs. It can be a formidable barrier to a couple holding contradictory or mutually exclusive views of God. A good place to deal with divergent views is right in the contract.

Ideally, both mates will develop the ability to see that different views exist. Trying to understand them may be frightening. "How does my faith coexist with others?" If that overwhelms the inquirer (or causes intolerable tension between the spouses), the inquirer may either move toward disillusionment —"There must not be a true God"—or toward rigidity. Rigidity is blind, unthinking adherence to either the faith of the family of origin or a totally new cultic belief. This Second Passage is a very common time when couples gravitate toward cults.

When writing your new contract, you'll want to address the particulars of your own spiritual life:

My view of God: _____

_____

My spouse's view of God: _____

_____

Our common appreciation of God: _____

_____

Areas in which we can compromise or yield regarding God: _

_____

_____

My attitude toward Scripture: _____
My spouse's: _____
Areas of common ground: _____
My attitude toward Jesus Christ: _____

_____

My spouse's: _____

_____

Our common ground: _____
My other views of faith and religion: _____

_____

_____

My spouse's: _____

_____

_____

Our mutual statement of faith and commitment: _____

_____

_____

_____

_____

_____

Sexual Matters

If you want to minimize sexual difficulties and differences, resolve your other control issues in your contract—time, money, and all—for they will spill over into your bedroom. As we saw before, sexual dysfunction may be a symbolic battle reflecting deeper control battles. Of course, each blames the other. So very often we receive a case where the wife, unable to reach orgasm, blames him for being too insensitive, as he blames her for being too uptight, and they're actually fighting over other issues.

Sexual difficulties, therefore, exist on two levels: as a reflection of other control battles and as battles in their own right. To address this, we urge a two-pronged attack, and it can be written right into the new contract. First, the couple needs to be aware of the other control issues and talk them through prior to writing them out. Second, they need to compromise on the sexual differences themselves.

Mary Alice Minirth puts it this way: the bedroom door swings both ways. As other issues enter, so can compromise in the bedroom exit to smooth the way in other areas. Dr. Hemfelt says, "What goes on in the living room has dramatic impact on what happens in the bedroom, and what happens in the bedroom can aggravate or alleviate what goes on in the living room."

This Second Passage is a time of high vulnerability for an affair. In the Second Passage, an affair usually represents a flight away from intimacy. Here is the poor married man or woman, struggling with control issues, financial and career pressures, kids, and, in some, a fear of true intimacy. An affair offers an easy pseudo-intimacy—intimacy with no strings. The new love approves of the harried married person and accepts him or her without conditions. No one worries about who takes out the garbage or who handles finances. Control issues aren't a problem. Persons involved in an affair need not deal with boredom and everyday minor crises. That's the hard work of marriage. Yet these issues create a special, rich kind of intimacy.

Wise marital contractors therefore write a pledge of fidelity into their promises. Will that thwart the chances of an affair? Of course not. But it reduces them by putting in visible, solid, immutable writing the couple's promise to each other. It reminds, it encourages, it supports.

In the case of Tom and Marsha, where Marsha had an extramarital affair and Tom really never forgave her for it, they both had to pound out a new fidelity pledge. Once this was done, Tom found it easier to trust Marsha—she had committed to faithfulness at least in writing. Marsha no longer had to constantly prove her fidelity; the new contract relieved a lot of that pressure. Their situation shows how valuable a new contract can be. Somehow when the commitment is put in writing, it is more concrete.

We suggest each spouse write a contract independently, working out his and her new agenda and tasks. The first drafts may be similar for both or quite different. What one sees as a big-ticket item may not be significant to the other. One might want better financial boundaries while the other places better team parenting as the top priority.

Write down whatever you think it takes to move along through the passage and meet the needs of both of you.

Once the contracts are drafted we ask the couples to enter the negotiation phase, which like any arbitration involves some give-and-take.

Ian: "I need sexual fulfillment."

Rhoda: "Be specific."

Ian: "Intimacy several times a week. No nervousness, no embarrassment. Openness. Some experimentation."

Rhoda: "I can't offer all that—at least not yet. I request in my contract aloneness at least three nights a week and a date night at least once a week, something romantic."

Ian pondered all this a while. "Are we really serious about this contract business? Like a union? You know, unions are the thing in Australia. Everything's union, union contract. Are we doing that here? Like negotiating?"

"Yeah, I guess so."

"And it's going to be binding?"

"I suppose it has to be if it's going to work at all."

Ian nodded, delighted. He wrote down each very specific request on two slips of paper. He gave her hers and kept his. "When unions bargain, they trade off, this concession for that. Now how shall we trade?"

Rhoda was not a born negotiator. She was afraid to give and hesitant to get, lest her hopes be crushed if the promises were broken. She caught on, though, in a hurry. They traded slips and clung to slips and revised slips. In the end they each wrote a contract, which was in effect a binding promise to the other, based on the slips they held at the finish. The contract would be good for one calendar year, at which time negotiations would reopen. Ian wasn't a union man for nothing.

Your statement of fidelity: _____

_____

_____

Your requests regarding sexual needs: _____

_____

Your spouse's needs and requests: _____

_____

The final contract statement, reflecting needs and requests, as agreed to by both: _____

_____

_____

_____

_____

_____

_____

Give-and-take in open negotiation is an excellent way to work around strongly differing agendas. Parenting, for example, rarely means the same thing to both spouses. Your spouse thinks if you don't tightly discipline a child there will be grief to pay; you tend to feel a little coddling doesn't hurt. You're on different agendas, so it is best to make some adjustments. And you don't have to have kids yet. This is something best negotiated even before the first child arrives (or puppy—some people practice on puppies! The Hemfelts did). Marriages tend to fall apart when the kids come, because of the confusing agendas. It helps immensely to have some good strong shoring in place before the storm strikes.

We have displayed an example of a new marriage contract on page 171. Use it as a guide, but feel free to modify it for your own unique situations.

The Goals of Contracts

The bottom line of your marriage contract is the bottom line of any of Ian's union contracts—two entities helping each other succeed and move forward. The antithesis of dysfunction, in marriage as in anything else, is mutual aid, as each helps the other satisfy needs and complete the necessary tasks of each passage.

It is not a goal of the new contract that all parties agree on the same agenda. You may well reach the decision that you have different agendas and different priorities. Matching or meshing diverse agendas in which all parties prosper is just as fine as identical agendas, and perhaps even better.

Be aware that not all meshing agendas are wholesome. These two agendas, for instance, fit:

He: I believe all women should be submissive.

She: I believe all men should be dictatorial.

But no one's going to grow in that relationship. The love, then the respect, and eventually perhaps even the marriage itself, will die.

An example in our counseling recently illustrates unwholesome meshing of agendas. A husband wanted to carve out a vocational identity for himself and the wife declared a contract in which security was the top priority. Those two agendas could mesh nicely, as he built the security of a strong presence on the job. But they became antagonistic, for he spent long hours on overtime and she languished, uncertain of his love. Her concept of security was emotional, his monetary.

One result of clear communication and honest contract negotiation is improved intimacy. You know each other better, understand each other better, appreciate each other better. You can better grasp what makes your marriage tick. You can see harmful influences and work out ways together to combat them. You can see the healthy, positive influences and rejoice in them. Just the act of building a mutually advantageous contract can bind you together more securely.

This concept of contract writing is not a quick fix for anything. You have to do the homework first, all of it. If you haven't dug out hidden agendas, the surface patch-up will surely fail.

Consider Loren and Gayle, a couple who always fought. They both had intense but perfectly coordinated hidden agendas. Both said, "I'm marrying you so I can have a sparring partner." Unfortunately, a serious case of denial kicked in, and neither would accept what their hidden agendas really were. The agendas remained hidden. Any new contract they negotiated set them up to fail because the underlying agreement made fighting inevitable. With new contracts they simply found different things to fight about.

Most people recognize that shallow counseling isn't going to work, even if they don't know why. This is why: They didn't do the groundwork.

Grace and Ron Chevington were at this crossroad. They had decided to enter counseling, but they had not started the groundwork. Their marriage, which was very, very sick, needed lots of help. Shallow counseling wouldn't do the job. They had to be willing to work at their marriage diligently, decide that it was worth the effort. Neither had made that decision yet. What could happen if Ron wanted to make the effort and Grace did not?

When One Side Refuses

Joe did a reverse intervention on Barbara to get her back into counseling (this, incidentally, is a very common situation).

An intervention is not a bright, snappy silver bullet to cure whatever motivational problem a loved one may have. It's a painful, carefully orchestrated, serious tool, not to be taken lightly. In this case, Joe and Brian gathered friends and associates who understood the importance of AA and were seeing troubling mood changes in Barbara. Several had passed through that same crisis themselves. They were coached so as to convey their concern in loving ways. At the appointed time, they arrived at Joe and Barbara's, sat down in the living room, and one by one voiced to Barbara their worries and cares about her loss of happiness. They enumerated very specific instances which indicated the unhealthy changes they saw in her behavior. Together they urged her into counseling, not for Joe's sake but for her own. A boss, the children—had Barbara any of those, they would logically have been included.

But what if Barbara had refused?

In so many marriages, one partner focuses on change and improvement but the other has no interest or may even sabotage it, desperately afraid of change. Then what?

It is *not* true that a marriage can't change for the better unless both spouses buy into the change.

Because we already know quite a bit about Joe and Barbara, and their interior motivations, let's use them in a hypothetical case. Let's pretend Barbara backed off and clung to her old dysfunctional attitudes. She would tend the wounded bird whether he wanted tending or not. She would continue trying to fix what her mother and grandmother could not, even if it already fixed itself. She would not give up control (this is not so hypothetical after all; frequently, spouses in our counsel flatly refuse to cooperate).

In that case, Joe would draw up a new contract stating "How I am choosing to be in this marriage." This automatically cancels the dysfunctional contract between Barbara and him. So, as Joe persists in his new sobriety and comes to better understand the nature of his addiction and his recovery, he can change their relationship—*to an extent*—by abandoning the dysfunctional contract.

Invitation to the Dance

Let's illustrate that in a different light through a woman we'll call Katherine. Because of the tendency to polarize we've discussed throughout this book, Katherine took on more and more jobs in her marriage that, to an increasing extent, didn't get done if she left them to her husband, Glen. Eventually she was handling the checkbook, the income tax, the mortgage payments, social scheduling, and all medical and legal appointments—not to mention mowing the lawn. Glen didn't deliberately avoid those things; he simply didn't get around to them. Angry and frustrated, she turned to a reliable friend, a friend who didn't seem to have that problem, for advice.

The friend suggested that Katherine consider a stalemate. Katherine mulled that advice carefully. It seemed sound, so she acted. "I created a crisis," she later explained. "No, that's not quite it. I let the crisis happen. First I decided what I absolutely wanted to get done. That was appointments involving the kids, income tax, and the mortgage payment. I made certain those things were kept current.

"I told Glen I was handing the rest back to him. Instead of watching sports on TV all night, he could balance the checkbook and some of those things. 'I will no longer do them,' I said. He shrugged it off; I don't think he thought I was serious.

"Chaos. I mean, there was chaos. The checkbook was a mess. He got billed for a dental appointment he made and forgot. He showed up twenty-four hours late to his boss's hot tub party. The lawn grew so high we kept losing the dog. I stood firm. 'You take some of the responsibility in this outfit,' I told him. 'It's supposed to be a two-person operation.'

"Eventually, it was. I think the turning point was when the bank called him at work and threatened to repossess his pickup truck if he didn't pay up by the close of that day. He delivered the check in person."

Katherine smiles now. "But I was tearing my hair out by then. It was a learning experience for me too. Now I know that even when only one person forges a new contract, and enforces it, it saps the strength of the old one."

Katherine invited her partner back into the dance. In essence she was doing what Al-Anon and other codependency groups have long advocated: Quit enabling. When one person decides not to enable, the other must change. Even if the other party doesn't buy into the new arrangement, crisis develops, and that crisis will force the other party to address the dysfunctional contract.

Ian would have explained it another way. "You're talking

about a contract walkout. Union and management are forced to negotiate. The union or company may walk out of contract negotiation if they don't see progress. That's not walking out of the company. The person is not walking out of the marriage, right? Just the situation. When you're on strike, mate, something's got to give!"

Strike the Band

Unfortunately, we find strikes happening in marriages all the time, often at the subconscious level, down on the level of those hidden agendas. They are not engaged for constructive purposes, such as the strike Katherine used to advantage, and if they go unrecognized, they may last the balance of the marriage.

A very common strike we find is the woman who goes on strike sexually. "I'm cooking for you and doing your laundry. But no eroticism." A common way for the husband to go on strike is to stop participating in family affairs. "I'm the breadwinner, and I'm still here," but not at the little league game, the family picnic, or whatever. Usually if one or the other party is on strike, it has something to do with unresolved, unfinished anger, which is why we discussed how to resolve anger and practice forgiveness in our last chapter. If this is not done, any new contract will be just a paper-exercise in futility. Anger resolved and redirected in a positive way is healthy.

Katherine's strike was born of anger, but her strike was not an end in itself, and certainly not intended to punish Glen for wrongs real or imaginary. Her goal was healthy change. A strike without such a goal is futile and destructive.

If your marriage has sufficiently progressed and your new marriage contract has been invoked, you may be ready to leave the Second Passage. But first let's examine whether you have successfully mastered the tasks of this reality phase.

The Renewed Marriage Contract

1. Statement of affirmation; at least one attribute each person admires and appreciates in the other

2. Statement of extent of commitment to the marriage

3. Promise of fidelity

4. Statement of faith, embracing:
   a. Each person's individual statement of faith
   b. Clearly stated common ground
   c. Statement of tolerance (and limits of tolerance)

5. Statement of recognition of old, dysfunctional hidden agendas

6. Declaration of new agendas to redress dysfunctions

7. Sexual contract, including:
   a. Recognition of difficulties or shortcomings in present sexual relations
   b. Steps to improve relations and/or explore new techniques
   c. Details of frequency if frequency is an issue

8. Review of items in first contract, with updates and revisions as necessary

9. Details of everyday life (request for romantic nights out) established through give-and-take (be specific)

10. Agreement on matters associated with children, if appropriate

11. Agreement to review and update contract periodically (anniversaries for instance)

Chapter 10

How Well Have You Completed the Second Passage?

A s the children grow, the marriage continues its inexorable changes, from reality into comfort. You are slipping into the next passage much as you would slip into a comfy, familiar pair of old house slippers. If that's not poles apart from the romance with which your union started, what is? It's worth considering in detail, this Third Passage, for it will shape what is to come and can renew that which passed.

But to get there, you must have completed the Second Passage. Take some time to participate in the following exercises. The Newmans use these when evaluating a couple's marriage progress. Share and enjoy these activities as a couple.

1. Write out ten negative characteristics of your spouse (each of you):

    1) _____

    2) _____

    3) _____

    4) _____

    5) _____

    6) _____

    7) _____

    8) _____

9) _____
10) _____

Now go back over the list and write out at least two positive characteristics beside each negative characteristic. Then fill in the following sentences:

I was surprised by my list because . . .

_____
_____

It's easier to be negative about my mate because . . .

_____
_____

2. Write out ten characteristics of your father in the space below:

3. Write out ten characteristics of your mother in the space below:

4. Look at the two lists above and write any characteristics that
your spouse shares with your parents in the space below:

Expectation Exercise

1. Describe the man/woman you dreamed of marrying when
you were single or a child.

_____

_____

2. What are the five most important expectations you had and/
or have now of your mate?

1) _____

2) _____

3) _____

4) _____

5) _____

3. Do you see anything in those expectations that's unrealistic?
Ask your husband or wife to review the list of expectations you
have of them.

4. Now, what are some more realistic expectations you can
have of each other?

1) _____

2) _____

3) _____

4) _____
5) _____

Romance Exercise

Write a love letter to your spouse and send it to him/her at their place of work (home if necessary).

Things to Avoid

Brian and Debi Newman have compiled some tidbits of information to help you avoid some of the pitfalls we've discussed so far in this book. Each of these are designed to get you thinking how to hogtie them before they get the best of you and your marriage.

Getting Involved in an Emotional or Sexual Affair

1. What has been the hardest reality you have had to face about marriage?

_____
_____

2. How would this reality still be true if you were married to someone else?

_____
_____

Putting Your Children above Your Marriage

1. How many hours a week do you spend one-on-one with each other? _____

2. How many dates without children have you had this month? _____

3. Do you have time together, alone at least three times a week?

_____

4. What are your priorities regarding your relationship with God, your spouse, your children, your job, and the church? _____

Debi explains, from personal experience, "Early in our marriage, before children, Brian and I found that we needed to take at least one weekend alone each year. We either went to a

Marriage Enrichment event (which we were not leading) or we took a vacation alone together. Now that we have children, these weekends alone have proven even more valuable. They are an important time to renew our love and recommit ourselves to each other. Many times Brian and I stop liking each other because we only see the pressured, angry personality. When we take off that pressure, we find a whole new personality that we love."

How about using the opportunity to do these exercises, take these quizzes, or even renew a marriage contract as a reason for a weekend getaway?

Putting Your Career above Your Marriage and/or Your Family

Dr. Minirth puts the commitment against this pitfall another way: "Early on, both mates must consciously say and practice, 'Our marriage and family are more important than my career, my friends, and my family-of-origin.'"

1. Is any member of the family showing signs of stress?

_____ yes _____ no

2. Have you had a family vacation this year? (when, where, how long)

_____

_____

3. Put the following list in priority order, with one being the most important:

_____ Promotion at Work

_____ Parenting

_____ Personal Relationship with God

_____ Marriage

_____ Relatives

_____ Friends

_____ Purchasing Home

_____ Some Type of Worship

_____ Physical Fitness

_____ Entertainment, Fun

Trying to Change Your Spouse

Beware of trying to change your spouse for your benefit. Work through the following questions to see if you're consciously or subconsciously doing just that.

1. List the qualities of your spouse that you want to change.

_____

_____

Even though Debi Newman didn't like Brian's domineering personality at first, like the radio incident in their apartment, she came to appreciate it. "After being married to Brian for seven years, I now have a much stronger personality. If Brian wasn't so domineering, I would never have become more assertive."

And Brian Newman admits that some of Debi's qualities he found distasteful at first have actually improved his. "I realized I was too uptight about having things clean and tidy. The shoe incident taught me to relax my standards a little. Now, seven years later, I'm the one who leaves my shoes lying around. And, I'm a little more mellow. It's a real plus now that we have children—who are whizzes at creating clutter."

2. Describe how those qualities improve you personally and/or improve your relationship:

_____

_____

Growing Apart—Passing in the Night

1. Do you know the most significant book or saying your spouse has read lately? _____yes _____no. What is it?

_____

2. Do you know your husband or wife's latest favorite outfit? _____yes _____no. What is it?_____

3. Do you know the person who has hurt your spouse the most this past week? _____yes _____no. Who is it? _____

4. Do you know the person who has most encouraged your mate this past week? _____yes _____no. Who is it? _____

5. What is your spouse's greatest fear?

_____

If you can answer "no" to one of the above questions, you are both probably growing apart and need to find each other again. (Before making this assumption, you might want to check with your spouse to see if your answers are correct.) We also recommend your spouse participate in these exercises—separately. Then you can reconnect with each other to see how well you've both faired.

Too Tired for Sex

This is a real biggie for the next passage (Third Passage). Nip this in the bud before it gets out of hand.

1. How often have you had sex this week? _____ This month? _____ This year? _____
What is your comment on the above observations? _____

_____

_____

Obviously, what is often enough for one marriage might not be for another. There will be differences between couples. The key is that you must both be satisfied with your sexual relationship.

Another arena you must both be satisfied with is your spiritual lives. You must be careful not to make this an area of conflict by being afraid of each other's beliefs.

Threatened by Each Other's Spiritual Life

Again, Brian and Debi Newman can speak from personal experience. Debi explains, "Brian wanted a family altar in our home ever since we first got married. To be honest, the vision of this sort of thing, the way he described it, was never appealing to me.

"One day I got this great idea. I told him I would make a tablecloth for our dining room table with special verses and it could be our family altar."

"Well, that wasn't what I had in mind at all," Brian remembers. "Over the years, I kept at my dream, consulting church furniture companies, having friends and relatives on the lookout for a used one. Finally, I found an antique one from a church. It was smaller than what I had in mind, but I bought it anyway."

Debi continues, "I was worried. Where were we going to

put the thing? How would it fit in with our decor? How could we afford it? But when I saw how critical it was to Brian, I gave in on this one.

"Know what? Our daughter, Rachel loves it. I have even found myself praying on it over and over. I'm really glad I didn't put my foot down on this issue."

Now, give your mate permission to pursue his/her spiritual needs. You can fill in the following:

I, _____, give you permission to grow in God at your own pace. You can share with me as you feel open; I will share my walk with you and not expect you to do what I do.

_____   _____
Signature   Date

You can even make this permission part of your new contract we discussed in the last chapter.

Are the Tasks of This Passage Complete?

If your marriage has progressed in years and/or maturity to the point of entering the Third Passage, take the following test to see how well you survived and learned from the Second Passage. The Newmans actually use this in counseling to see whether a couple has passed second base, in essence, and are on their way to third. We suggest that each of you go through this evaluation separately and then discuss your results together. (We even give you permission to xerox this part of the book for this very purpose!)

Each of the statements are organized under the specific tasks we've discussed so far. Check those that apply to you. Again we invite you to make your own assessment and make any adjustments in your marriage that seem possible.

The First Task: Hang On to Love After Reality Strikes

_____ I've learned a lot of new things about my spouse, and not all of them have been positive.

_____ I forgive my mate on a daily basis.

_____ Some days I act lovingly to my husband/wife even though he/she doesn't deserve it.

_____ I can still find characteristics about my spouse that I appreciate.

_____ I make a conscious effort to be kind to my wife/husband.

_____ We maintain a healthy and consistent sexual relationship.

_____ I have learned that happily-ever-after doesn't come naturally.

_____ I can honestly say that I have accepted my spouse, warts and all.

_____ I don't always like my mate, but I choose to love her/him.

_____ I have changed my personality style or personal habits to please my husband/wife and I don't resent it.

_____ I can talk honestly and openly about the personality characteristics or personal habits that I don't like in my spouse.

_____ I am willing to give a love gift to my mate, by ending an argument his/her way once in a while.

_____ Our marriage has hit some ups and downs, but I feel we are stronger and closer than when we were first married.

_____ We have managed to find a routine for household chores where neither of us is doing all or most of the work and we vary the responsibilities for those chores from time to time.

_____ I must say the rose-colored glasses have come off in my view of my spouse, but I'm going to commit to this marriage anyway.

Looking back over your and your spouse's responses to these statements, can you see any areas that need adjustment? Help? Communication with each other? As a very general rule of thumb, if a couple cannot check at least ten of these statements, they may need to work on accepting and appreciating the reality of their lives together.

The Second Task: Childproof Your Marriage

_____ We have children, or we agree on when to start our family, or whether we will have children at all.

_____ We are able to meet our financial obligations.

_____ We agree on our philosophy of child rearing.

_____ We have talked about the number and the best timing for children.

_____ We make time for ourselves alone at least two times a month.

_____ We are able to leave our children for a few hours with a trusted adult.

_____ We sit down to eat at least five meals a week at our own dinner table as a family.

_____ We have found ways to keep a healthy, active sexual relationship in spite of the children.

_____ We offer a stable marriage for the children to grow up in.

_____ We don't lean on the children for support or try to ask them to take sides in our arguments.

_____ My partner comes first before the children.

_____ If we want children and haven't been able to have them, we support each other through the grieving process.

_____ I've realized that parenting is not an easy task.

_____ We have times for family outings that are enjoyable for everyone.

_____ We balance our children's schedules on their behalf and don't overcommit them, even for worthwhile activities.

How well do you and your spouse agree on raising children and your marriage's priority? Can you both check most of these statements—particularly the one about putting each other above the children? If not, you may need to work out those "parenting" issues before they mess up your marriage. They undoubtedly will if you don't childproof it.

The Third Task: Recognize the Hidden Contracts in Your Marriage

_____ I have discovered some of the similarities in my spouse and my family of origin.

_____ I've realized some of the reasons I really married my husband/wife that put a lot of pressure on him/her.

_____ I'm not carrying on the battle of the sexes in our marriage.

_____ I accept that I had unrealistic expectations of my spouse.

_____ I want to find the hidden contracts in our marriage and get them in the open.

_____ I'm willing to admit if I find a destructive hidden contract, I will try to get rid of it.

_____ I can see how damaging hidden contracts can be to a marriage.

_____ Some of our fights have resulted from unreal expectations of each other.

_____ I'm willing to lower my expectations of my spouse.

_____ There are some facets of my mate that are better than I even expected when I met him/her.

_____ I'm not trying to fix my parents' marriage with my current marriage.

Did you and your spouse find that hidden contracts were at work in your marriage? If you couldn't check most, if not all, of these statements, they probably are. We fully endorse professional counseling if these hidden agendas seem prevalent and damaging.

The Fourth Task: Write a New Marriage Contract

_____ We have sat down as a couple and written our renewed marriage contract.

_____ I realize happily-ever-after takes work and I'm willing to work at loving my wife/husband.

_____ I promise to be faithful to my spouse both sexually and emotionally.

_____ A reachable expectation I have of my mate is:

_____

_____ A reachable expectation I have of myself is:

_____

_____ Something I expected of our marriage, but didn't realize is: _____.
I would like to make this expectation part of our renewed contract.

_____ We have scheduled time alone so we can help our marriage grow.

_____ I have made some compromises in our relationship.

_____ I'm willing to do everything I can to negotiate and set up a new marriage contract.

_____ I take the renewed contract we made seriously. It is not just an activity.

_____ My spouse can count on my promises.

_____ I realize this renewed contract will eventually become obsolete and we will have to draft another one for the benefit of our marriage.

_____ I'm currently satisfied with the issues we raised in this renewed contract.

_____ I'm willing to cross off any hidden agendas from this contract.

_____ I'm willing to participate honestly as we renew our marriage contract. I am not just doing it to please my spouse.

_____ I am fully committed to this marriage.

If you and your spouse could check almost all of these statements, you are on your way to successfully completing the Second Passage. If not, you both may need more negotiation on major contractual items we discussed in Chapter 9. Writing a new contract assures completion of one passage and a full embrace of the next one.

Somewhere around the tenth anniversary, the couple will recognize another shift in their relationship. Usually this marks the commencement of the Third Passage. Like the Second, the Third Passage has its own set of tasks and challenges that can avoid disaster and ultimately lead to greater marital enrichment.

Beyond the Third Passage, lurks the Fourth and the Fifth—each providing more tasks and challenges, and each pointing the way to home base—the score, the goal! Page 187 shows what lies ahead for the couple as they make their way towards home plate amid the cheering crowd. Third base is their next stop.

Looking Ahead to the Third Passage

Kayla loved these informal, Thursday night pick-up volleyball games. You never knew who was going to show up at the community center here, but it was always an interesting team. The guy across the net spiked his set-up and Len, beside Kayla, dived and saved it. He popped it straight up and Kayla moved in under the ball.

She heard the thunder of male feet coming at her from behind. She braced and ignored them for now. The moment the ball touched her hands and she sent it back over the net, she swung behind her with her elbow—and caught Rollie right in the breadbasket.

Keeping her eye on the ball in the far court, she yelled without turning. "Rollie, you dork, don't do that again! You handle your position and quit charging mine!"

The three other women on the team clapped and cheered.

After the game, Rollie drew Kayla aside. "Sorry about coming on you like that. I guess I tend to do that. But your back was turned. How'd you know it was me?"

"Apology accepted. Your shoes. Anyone else coming up behind me would sound like thump-thump. You're thump-slap thump-slap. Why don't you save your pennies and buy a pair of real shoes, instead of those old things with the loose sole flapping? You splack every time you take a step."

He looked down at his grey and battered gym sneakers, at the cracks across the arches, at the green paint spots, at the holes where he accidentally dribbled battery acid. "I don't know. They're old friends. They're comfortable. I'm used to them." He smiled. "I guess when I look at them I still see them like when they were new."

Old friends. Comfortable. Used to them. Selective vision. Rollie might as well have been describing a marriage in its Third Passage. Like Rollie's old shoes, the married couple feel comfortable, familiar, even complacent. They tend to take each other for granted, not for lack of love but simply because each can thoroughly anticipate what the other will do and say.

Rollie's mind's eye saw his shoes as still new. In their minds' eyes, the married couple still harbor the deeply buried dream of a perfect union, a perfect mate, a perfect romance. And like Rollie's shoes, reality does not match in the least the vision.

But a curious thing also happens in this Third Passage of marriage. In spite of the familiarity and comfort, true intimacy often dwindles. The couple drift apart, each totally wrapped up in his and her special sphere—kids, job, getting ahead, keeping up, coping, making do.

Picture a wheel. At the top is interdependence, the ideal. Each person is his own, her own, and yet they depend upon each other for certain needs and wants. Label the three-o'clock side of the wheel "Exaggerated independence." Here are two people going their separate ways, moving farther and farther apart. Eventually they will find themselves antagonistic toward each other, or simply so out of touch that the marriage seemingly doesn't matter anymore.

Label the other, the nine o'clock side, "Exaggerated dependence." The couple sliding down this side are so enmeshed they are losing their individual identities—not a healthy situation. Sooner or later, one will be lost. One may feel so suffocated by the relationship that he or she will leave it. This exaggerated dependence also leads to antagonism and conflict as the couple jockey for more and more attention. They irritate each other more and more, as the too-tight relationship chafes and pinches. Pretty much like shoes.

Also by this stage, it is beginning to dawn on each partner that some (perhaps all) aspirations of youth will never be met. It is a time of mourning—lost youth, lost vigor, lost comeliness, lost dreams.

Toss into that volatile pot the kids, who in their adolescence are working on their own problems of separation and individuation. This is the most friction-filled period of growth and development in kids and therefore for the Third-Passage family as well.

Hopeless? Hardly! Rollie's shoes need to see a shoemaker; at the very least he ought to buy a roll of duct tape for them; but they ought not be given up as lost. After all, they've seen a lot of miles, they still serve well (once the splack is fixed), and they really are marvelously comfortable—steadfast, worth saving, by all means. As is any marriage.

But then, that's another book in itself.

Major Tasks of All the Passages of Marriage

THE FIRST PASSAGE–NEW LOVE
(The First Two Years of Marriage)

Task 1: Mold into One Family
Task 2: Overcome the Tendency to Jockey for Control
Task 3: Build a Sexual Union
Task 4: Make Responsible Choices
Task 5: Deal with Your Parents' Incomplete Passages

THE SECOND PASSAGE–REALISTIC LOVE
(From the Second through the Tenth Anniversary of Marriage)

Task 1: Hang On to Love After Reality Strikes
Task 2: Childproof Your Marriage
Task 3: Recognize the Hidden Contracts in Your Marriage
Task 4: Write a New Marriage Contract

THE THIRD PASSAGE–STEADFAST LOVE
(From the Tenth Anniversary through the Twenty-fifth)

Task 1: Maintain an Individual Identity along with the Marriage Identity
Task 2: Say the Final Good-byes
Task 3: Overcome the Now-or-Never Syndrome
Task 4: Practice True Forgiveness
Task 5: Accept the Inevitable Losses
Task 6: Help Your Adolescent Become an Individual
Task 7: Maintain an Intimate Relationship

THE FOURTH PASSAGE–RENEWING LOVE
(From the Twenty-fifth Anniversary through the Thirty-fifth)

Task 1: Combat the Crisis of This Passage
Task 2: Reestablish Intimacy
Task 3: Grieve the Particular Losses of This Passage

THE FIFTH PASSAGE–TRANSCENDENT LOVE
(Beyond the Thirty-fifth Anniversary)

Task 1: Prepare for Retirement
Task 2: Continue Renewing Love
Task 3: Achieve a Transcendent Perspective
Task 4: Accept My One and Only God-given Life

Dr. Frank Minirth is a diplomate of the American Board of Psychiatry and Neurology. Along with Dr. Paul Meier, he founded the Minirth-Meier Clinic in Dallas, Texas, one of the largest psychiatric clinics in the United States.

Mary Alice Minirth is a homemaker and the mother of four children.

Dr. Brian Newman is the clinical director of inpatient services at the Minirth-Meier Clinic in Richardson, Texas. He received his M.A. in counseling from Grace Theological Seminary and his Doctorate of Philosophy from Oxford Graduate School.

Dr. Deborah Newman is a psychotherapist with the Minirth-Meier Clinic. She received her M.A. in counseling from Grace Theological Seminary and her Doctorate of Philosophy from Oxford Graduate School.

Dr. Robert Hemfelt is a psychologist with the Minirth-Meier Clinic who specializes in the treatment of chemical dependencies and compulsivity disorders.

Susan Hemfelt is a homemaker and the mother of three children.